WHAT LINNAEUS SAW

WHAT LINNAEUS SAW

SAW

A Scientist's Quest
to Name Every Living Thing

KAREN
MAGNUSON BEIL

◇◇

Norton Young Readers

An Imprint of W. W. Norton & Company
Independent Publishers Since 1923

For information about permission to reproduce selections from this book, write to Permissions, W. W. Norton & Company, Inc., 500 Fifth Avenue, New York, NY 10110

For information about special discounts for bulk purchases, please contact W. W. Norton Special Sales at specialsales@wwnorton.com or 800-233-4830

Manufacturing by Worzalla
Book design by Jen Montgomery
Production manager: Julia Druskin

Library of Congress Cataloging-in-Publication Data

Names: Beil, Karen Magnuson, author.
Title: What Linnaeus saw : a scientist's quest to name every living thing / Karen Magnuson Beil.
Description: New York, NY : Norton Young Readers, an imprint of W.W. Norton & Company, [2019] | Audience: Age 10–14. | Includes bibliographical references and index.
Identifiers: LCCN 2019014206 | ISBN 9781324004684 (hardcover)
Subjects: LCSH: Linné, Carl von, 1707–1778—Juvenile literature. | Naturalists—Sweden—Biography—Juvenile literature.
Classification: LCC QH44 .B45 2019 | DDC 508.092 [B] —dc23
LC record available at https://lccn.loc.gov/2019014206

W. W. Norton & Company, Inc., 500 Fifth Avenue, New York, N.Y. 10110
www.wwnorton.com

W. W. Norton & Company Ltd., 15 Carlisle Street, London W1D 3BS

1 2 3 4 5 6 7 8 9 0

For Kim and Pat

[Here is] what all children who wander in the woods know, without even realizing that they know it: the living world is not some random mess, but an array of clusters of more and less similar things.

—CAROL KAESUK YOON, *NAMING NATURE*

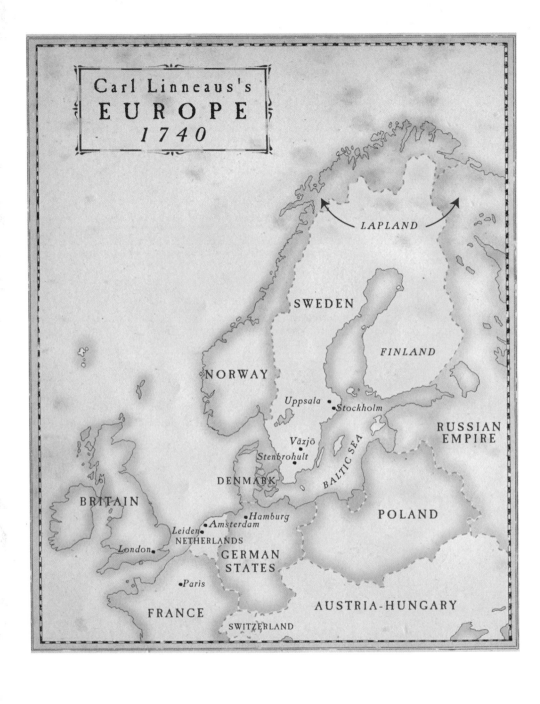

Carl Linneaus's
EUROPE
1740

LAPLAND

SWEDEN

FINLAND

NORWAY

Uppsala • *Stockholm*

RUSSIAN
EMPIRE

Växjö

Stenbrohult •

BALTIC SEA

DENMARK

BRITAIN

POLAND

• *Hamburg*
• *Amsterdam*

Leiden •
NETHERLANDS

GERMAN
STATES

London •

• *Paris*

AUSTRIA-HUNGARY

FRANCE

SWITZERLAND

CONTENTS

Carl Linnaeus

(pronounced lin-NAY-us)

May 23, 1707–January 10, 1778

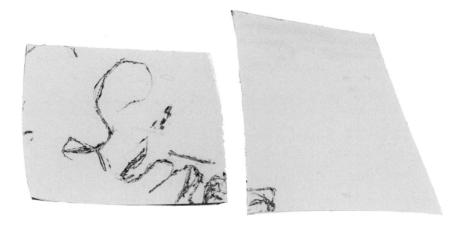

Carl Linnaeus scratched his name into the window of his room during his school year at Lund University in 1728-1729. (The line above the "n" doubles the letter below.) When the house was demolished years later, these glass fragments were discovered and preserved.

Introduction

<><><><><><><><><><><><><><><><><><><><><><><><><><><><><><><><><>

SJUPP'S STORY

If you do not know the names of things,
the knowledge of them is lost too.

—CARL LINNAEUS, *PHILOSOPHIA BOTANICA*
(THE SCIENCE OF BOTANY), 1751

The strange animal poked around the study, sniffing, searching. Carl Linnaeus watched for clues. Where did this little fellow fit in the animal kingdom? People had their theories. Was it a type of bear or badger? A canine? A cat? Or something else entirely? Nobody knew. At his desk, Linnaeus pored through books by other scientists for descriptions of the animal, its habitats, behaviors, economic uses, and names. One naturalist called the animal *Vulpi affinis americana*, linking it to the American red fox. Linnaeus examined a published drawing of another animal—smaller, thinner, and with a longer tail. He realized they were related, but that creature turned out to be a coati from South America.

Linnaeus's animal was not native to Sweden; in fact, it was

not native to any place in Europe. It had been brought over on a ship from North America. Most likely it was trapped by settlers along the Delaware River, where there once had been a small Swedish colony. The animal briefly lived the high life in the King's royal garden in Stockholm. Then, sometime in 1746 or 1747, Crown Prince Adolf Fredrik gave the creature to Linnaeus, the thirty-nine-year-old world-renowned scientist at Uppsala University. The prince had one royal request: figure out what it is.

Other unusual animals would live in the university's gardens—monkeys, parrots, peacocks—but this one quickly became the family's darling and lived in the house. They called it Sjupp, pronounced "shewp."

Having Sjupp living right there in the house made him hard to ignore and easy to observe, perfect for the busy professor, who noted:

— back feet are longer and broader than the front,

— walks on hind feet like a man or bear,

— stands somewhat larger than a cat, almost as big as a hare, but shorter and closer to the ground, and with a rounded back, like a bear

— hears poorly with small ears and requires a shout to get his attention,

— sees poorly,

— possesses keen senses of smell and touch. Locates even the smallest crumb tossed to him, not by seeing it but by sniffing and by patting the ground with his soft paws.

Sjupp liked to laze on his stomach and stretch out his legs. He was not interested in the shriveled-up plants from Sri Lanka that Linnaeus studied incessantly that summer; he'd rather have a ripe cherry. But as soon as Professor Linnaeus knocked the tobacco out of his pipe and tossed the cold pipe to the floor, Sjupp rose up on his hind legs and hustled over to pick it up. Squatting on his haunches, he gently rolled the smooth pipe stem between his paws. He could do this for hours.

He was a pickpocket and a thief, always on the wrong side of mischief. With slender flexible fingers and despite the inconvenience of not having thumbs, he managed to help himself to tasty treats. A sweet cake that Mrs. Linnaeus had hidden on top of the tall walnut cupboard. Eggs from nests in the yard. Terrified birds in the university's garden. Raisins and almonds right out of students' pockets.

This pampered pet ate richly—sugary cakes, meats, bread, porridge, apples, pears, lingonberries, cherries, strawberries, bird bones, raisins, crayfish, and eggs, anything except raw or boiled fish, or foods prepared with vinegar such as sauerkraut.

Sjupp wandered through the professor's upstairs library. Books, shells, rocks, bones, and packets of seeds folded like Japanese origami sat here and there. Hundreds of pressed plants glued onto paper were stacked on shelves labeled I to XXIV in three towering gray cabinets. Potted plants crowded the windowsill.

Through the open window, where birds flew in and out, the professor had a commanding view of the medical school's teaching garden. Sjupp caught a whiff from the window and

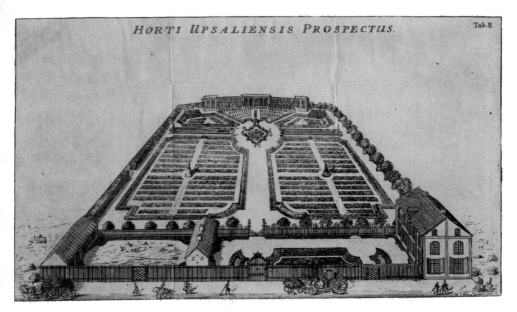

The Uppsala University teaching garden. Along the back was an orangery. This eighteenth-century greenhouse, precursor of today's all-glass structures, had large windows and was heated for growing delicate warm-climate plants, such as citrus trees. To the left of the garden gate were stables, a coach house, farm sheds, a henhouse, brewing house, and servants' quarters. To the right stood the two-story home of the medical professor, where the Linnaeus family lived.

let out a horrible squawk—a warning that the gardener was working below. On their first meeting, Sjupp had climbed the gardener's leg to investigate, but the man panicked and shook him off roughly. Now whenever Sjupp smelled the man's scent, he screamed like an angry seagull.

Linnaeus watched, amused by the antics, fascinated by the behaviors. Nature enthralled him both scientifically and emotionally. He made detailed notes for his eventual report to the prince. The animal was friendly with children and dogs that he knew; he rolled onto his back and let the children pull his fur, but when they lost interest and tried to walk away he hung onto their feet and badgered them to keep playing. As "obstinate as a knife grinder," the professor wrote.

The children—Carl, age six, named for his father, and Lisa Stina, four—played with Sjupp endlessly. So did the college students who poured in and out of the family's house. Students wanting to get close enough to pet this rare New World animal bribed him with raisins. If anyone made the mistake of trying to pick him up or lead him on a rope, he'd lie on the floor, flailing his legs defiantly. He'd bare his teeth and claws and growl like a bear.

When Linnaeus offered him an egg in the garden, Sjupp would roll it carefully between his paws, nibble a little hole, then suck out the contents. Any hen that ventured too close was a goner. He'd bite off its head, drink the blood, and leave the carcass behind. One day Linnaeus was distressed to find Sjupp enjoying a meal of an impressively feathered peacock. If Linnaeus dangled him upside down by the tail to coerce him to release his prey, Sjupp clenched his teeth, renewing his hold with the force of an iron trap. Only a pig's-bristle broom could scare him off.

◇◇◇

In September 1747, a new semester was beginning, and the Linnaeus family's yellow stucco house on Black Creek Gate bustled with the commotion of students. Rather than gathering in the university's formal lecture hall, they often met for plant demonstrations and private classes at their professor's home, where his natural history collections and medical garden were close at hand to illustrate points and settle debates. The large upper-story room was frequently so crowded that students had to sandwich into the hallway or listen from the stairs. Wherever they were, Sjupp had plenty to do checking all those pockets for snacks.

One night after the family had gone to bed, the nocturnal Sjupp went wandering. Instead of roaming the quiet house as he normally did until midnight, he found a way outside. The next morning, Linnaeus, his wife, children, and students called and searched for Sjupp.

Several days later they found his mangled body.

Sjupp had climbed the fence into another yard where, Linnaeus concluded, a dog had attacked and killed him.

Now to fulfill his promise to the Crown Prince, there was one last step.

Dr. Linnaeus needed to conduct a dissection of this animal that he had been so fond of. He slid a scalpel into Sjupp's fur. Just under the skin, he found a layer of fat two fingers thick. Beneath that, the omentum, the transparent membrane holding the stomach and other abdominal organs, was crosshatched "like a spider's web" with thin white ribbons of fat.

Linnaeus's notes describe sizes and shapes using comparisons but with no standard measurements—the fat was two fingers thick, the heart was the size of a large plum, the stomach no bigger than a hen's egg. The stomach's smallness surprised him given Sjupp's ability to pack away a big plate of food in only an hour.

He described the liver, gallbladder, kidneys, pancreas, and spleen. The intestines were held by a transparent membrane called a mesentery which, like the omentum, was crisscrossed with a net of thin veins of fat. He marveled at the neatly defined blood vessels on the heart. He described the canine teeth, molars, and incisors, and the thick, strong muscles of the mouth.

Besides the obvious injuries from Sjupp's fatal fight with the dog, Linnaeus saw three abnormalities. First, the eyes were as round as marbles. Since eyeballs with normal vision are oval-shaped, this excessive curvature explained why Sjupp had been so nearsighted. Second, his left eyeball was dried out and crusty like a husk, indicating to Linnaeus that Sjupp had been blind in that eye. Third, he found abscesses in the lungs starting to discharge pus. He realized then that even if Sjupp had avoided doing deadly battle with the dog, he would not have lived to old age. Antibiotics would not be discovered for another two centuries, so there was little available to treat the infection.

◇◇◇

Linnaeus delivered his report to colleagues and the Crown Prince at a meeting of the Royal Swedish Academy of Sciences. He had determined that this animal was a member of the bear family because of his shape, his sticking-up hair, the slender s-curved bone in his penis, and his vocalizations. Other bearlike traits included grasping objects with his front paws and occasionally walking long distances on his hind legs.

In North America, Swedish colonists called this animal an ispan, which was their interpretation of the word *espan*, from an Algonquin language spoken by the Lenape people living along the Delaware River. It meant "the one who scratches to get into things." The colonists called the animal's pelt a sjupp, derived from *ausup*, another native word for the animal. Trappers sold the tails for fashionable striped scarves and the pelts for coats and winter hats which were popular among Swedish farmers. The settlers also ate its meat. Linnaeus's friend Peter Collinson, a Quaker merchant and avid amateur naturalist in London, raved that, when raised on dumplings and sugar, its meat was "really fine eating," even better than lamb.

Linnaeus apparently had not heard of *arakun*, another version of the word used by Algonquin speakers a little farther to the south—or, as the Jamestown colonists thought they heard it, "a raccoon."

Seven years earlier, Linnaeus had named Sjupp's species *Ursus cauda elongata*, a Latin phrase meaning "long-tailed bear." At the time, he had not seen the species in person and had to rely on other people's descriptions. Now his close daily observations of Sjupp and the dissection convinced him that the name was correct. However, names assigned by humans change as scientific discoveries are made. The year after Sjupp was killed, Linnaeus's student Pehr Kalm was exploring North America. When Kalm said he'd observed these animals washing their food, his teacher responded by changing its name to *Ursus lotor*, Latin for "washing bear."

A watercolor sketch of Sjupp painted by student Lars Alstrin. It still hangs in Linnaeus's summer house at Hammarby, outside Uppsala.

◇◇◇

Beyond the high fence where Sjupp had escaped, and south of Uppsala, boats sailed in and out of Stockholm harbor on Sweden's east coast along the Baltic Sea. On Sweden's west coast, tall-masted ships jockeyed for dock space in Göteborg's big harbor on the North Sea. Beyond it stretched the vast Atlantic Ocean.

Every day, explorers set sail from Europe. Their countries were small and their limited natural resources overused, so Europeans charged around the globe in a rush to explore and exploit lands on other continents. While they were at it, they were eager to discover and collect plants, animals, and minerals—valuable natural resources—for kings, queens, and wealthy merchants and collectors back home. Everyone was hungry for the exotic. More ships arriving in European ports meant more crates and barrels of tea from India, coffee beans and cacao from the Americas, silks, porcelain, and spices from China—expensive imports, unknown plants and animals from the farthest parts of the world.

Meanwhile, excited scientists scrambled to name and claim the curious specimens as they came ashore. Each used his own methods and terminology. Every specimen was called by so many names, in so many languages, that nobody knew what was what. Scientists were overwhelmed.

Carl Linnaeus liked things to be orderly. Even as a boy, he'd been a habitual list-maker. As a pastor's son who had already become the world's most famous naturalist, he was thrilled to see nature's astounding variety flooding into nearby ports, waiting to be examined, described, named, and put in order.

He had a big dream—maybe an impossible dream—to name and catalog every living thing. In fact, he felt he had been chosen by God to reveal the Creator's original plan for life.

He was in a hurry. It was a big job for one lifetime. He wanted to organize the entire natural world: every plant, every mineral, every creature great and small, including the lovable raisin-robber who once felt for crumbs beneath his desk.

The curiosity that drove Carl Linnaeus started early—with the plants in his father's garden.

RACCOON UPDATE

Science is always tentative, a set of mysteries to be solved, moving from chaos to order, and making the unknown knowable. As new information comes in, old theories fall.

Pehr Kalm believed that raccoons dunked their food in water to wash it. Later, naturalists assumed this was because they lacked salivary glands. Today, scientists know that raccoons do have salivary glands, as well as highly developed nerves in their forepaws: handling food in water softens the skin on a raccoon's paws, making it even more sensitive and capable of finding and distinguishing food.

Linnaeus was not wrong about the animal being related to bears, even though his assumptions were limited to physical traits that he could see. Using DNA research, twentieth-century scientists traced the animal's genetic evolution and found that raccoons and bears shared a common ancestor.

1

<><><><><><><><><><><><><><><><><><><><><><><><><><><><><><><><><><>

NOT ONE PUMPKIN

. . . though we be confined to one spot, one
corner of the earth, we may examine the great
and various stores of knowledge, and therein
behold the immense domains of nature.

—CARL LINNAEUS, HIS FIRST LECTURE AS A PROFESSOR,
 "AN ORATION CONCERNING THE NECESSITY OF
 TRAVELING IN ONE'S OWN COUNTRY," 1741

Ever since he was old enough to walk and pull weeds, Carl
had helped his father in the garden. Now sixteen years
old, at home for summer vacation in 1723, he kept his eye on a
pumpkin plant. His father had great hopes for it.

Flowers and fruit trees stretched out in dizzying variety, more
than 220 different kinds. The garden belonged to the parsonage,
which stood next to the church in Stenbrohult, Sweden, where
Carl's family lived. His father, Nils Linnaeus, was the pastor,
and Carl himself was studying to join the clergy.

The land sloped toward a lake, the opposite bank rising
to a hilly ridge. At a time when only grand estates had lavish
ornamental gardens, this yard alongside the simple wooden

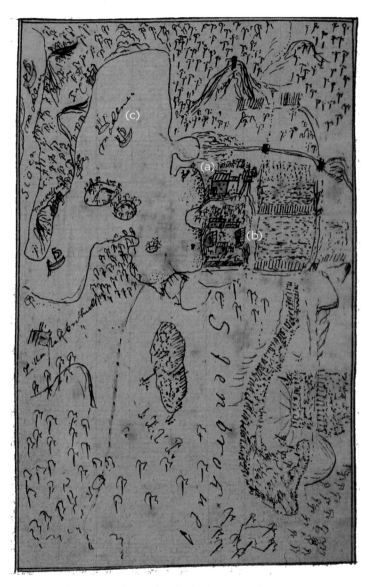

Carl sketched this map of Stenbrohult showing the parsonage where he grew up, his father's church (a), gardens (b), and Lake Möckeln (c). His father grew fruit trees including apples, pears, cherries, and plums; gooseberries, raspberries, and musk strawberries; vegetables such as turnips, artichokes, horseradish, spinach, and asparagus; flowers including tulips, daffodils, violets, and salvia; and rare trees including mulberry, fig, and dwarf almond.

parsonage was bursting with flowers and exotic trees, as well as practical "kitchen plants" to feed the family. Pastor Linnaeus's garden was said to be one of the best-stocked in this corner of Sweden.

Carl was happy to spend his summer here. At school, the boys—and even the masters—called him the Little Botanist. This garden was Carl's favorite place to be, a place where he routinely saw things that astonished him. And made him wonder . . .

The pumpkin plant—with its green vines, hairy leaves, and bright yellow flowers—looked as expected. Up close, with its prickly leaves pushed aside, he would have seen two kinds of flowers growing on the plant. One kind grew on a long, skinny stem. Inside its petals, several thread-like filaments clumped together as one, coated with a powdery yellow dust. The second kind of flower sat on a shorter, thicker stem with a berry-shaped bulge at its base. Inside that flower stood a short stalk with a sticky, bumpy crown on top. Nils taught his son the Latin names for these structures. Even there in the Swedish farm country, they knew that this North American plant typically had two different flowers, but they had no idea why those flowers were different or what their functions were.

At Nils's direction, every morning any new pumpkin flower with thread-like filaments, called stamens, was carefully snapped off. Any flower containing a short stalk, or pistil, with a bulge at its base was left to bloom. Experience growing other vines with two types of flowers, such as cucumbers and melons, had taught Nils that only the flowers with little green bulges at their bases would ripen and mature into fruits. So it seemed reasonable

An 1804 illustration showing cross-sections of two kinds of pumpkin flowers: on the left, with pistil and bulge, and on the right, with stamens fused together and no bulge.

to assume that removing the unwanted flowers would reduce competition for nutrients and cause the pumpkin plant to direct all its energy into the flowers with little green bulges.

Pumpkins were among the food plants important in Carl's mother's kitchen. His father's goal was to present her with a harvest of big pumpkins. Day after day for the rest of the summer, skinny-stemmed pumpkin flowers were beheaded. However, by summer's end, the garden revealed a puzzling result: no pumpkins. Not a single one.

It would be several years before Carl understood why his

A BRANCH OF THE FAMILY TREE

In the old Swedish name tradition, a child was given a first name plus a patronymic, which was derived from the father's first name. So Linnaeus would have been known as Carl, the son of Nils, or Carl Nilsson. His sister would have been called Anna Maria Nilsdotter (Anna Maria, the daughter of Nils). In a tiny village like Stenbrohult, that was all they'd need.

Children born into families who could afford education required a formal school name, to distinguish them from classmates whose names and patronymics might be the same as their own. This applied only to boys, because in the early eighteenth century, girls were rarely given the opportunity to go to school.

School names were often based on birthplace or nature. For instance, when Carl Linnaeus's father, Nils Ingemarsson, attended Lund University, he chose to call himself after a stately old linden tree on his family's farm. He took the tree's regional name, *lin*, added the Latinate ending *-aeus*, and became Nils Ingemarsson Linnaeus. Nils's child Carl was Carl Nilsson Linnaeus. When Carl married Sara Lisa Moraea, she retained her name, as was

father's pumpkin plants failed to make pumpkins that summer. Meanwhile, in September when the beech trees turned gold and days began to grow short, Carl had to leave once again. It had been nine summers since the day his parents first packed him off as a seven-year-old to the Växjö Cathedral School, to prepare him to follow his father into the clergy.

The thirty-mile trip took at least two days on horseback. The woods, the lake, the stony fields, and the garden with no pumpkins slipped into the distance as he made his way back to school alone.

the custom, but their children took their father's last name, his daughters' names ending in the feminine form, Linnaea.

When King Adolf Fredrik ennobled Carl Linnaeus in 1757 (it became official four years later), the professor adopted a new name: von Linné. Why he chose that name is not known, but it reflected the trend among the Swedish nobility toward all things French. Linnaeus provided a sketch upon which the royal herald based his coat of arms, designed to represent nature: "my little Linnaea in the helmet, with the shield divided into three fields: black, green, and red—the three kingdoms of Nature—superimposed on an egg." However, there was a dispute. Linnaeus's original sketch showed only the yellow yolk, and he was miffed when the royal herald misunderstood the symbolism and drew the entire egg.

Linnaeus made this sketch for his family coat of arms. The final design, created by the Swedish royal herald, is shown above.

◇◇

◇◇◇

Nearly three grueling years had passed since the summer of the failed pumpkins. Carl, now in the upper school at Växjö, was hiding an uncomfortable secret—he hated school. His grades proved it.

Every week of every year was the same routine—up before dawn for morning prayers and hymn singing, followed at 6 a.m. by classes, even on Saturdays. Every day four boys in four classes recited their lessons, shouting to be heard over one another, while their masters yelled corrections in a din of screaming, whipping, crying, and Latin practice. Teachers in those days were called masters; their students were disciples. "Brutal teachers used such brutal methods," as Carl described it later; this was the accepted teaching method, meant to inspire him to learn.

On sunny days, though, what it inspired Carl to do was skip his studies to head for the fields and the thing he enjoyed most— hunting for interesting plants. Any boy who misbehaved or was absent was sent to cut birch branches into switches with which the schoolmasters would "teach" him his lessons. Carl paid for these days off. But a day in the field was worth it. It was a survival tool.

Carl's notebook was probably a survival tool, too. Bound inside its soft blue and brown covers were 160 precious pages embossed with an Amsterdam watermark. A year ago, they'd been blank.

Now the pages were filling up, one plant per page, with no wasted space. At the top of each page he would write a plant's common name in Swedish, then a scientific name in Latin or Greek. Next came the name's origin, the plant's uses, description, toxicity, and habitat. Sometimes he included lore about the plant—proverbs, or stories from the Bible or from Greek or Roman mythology.

Any entries too long for one page he continued upside down on a page with a shorter entry. Since he added plants as he found them in the fields or in books, they were in no particular order, a hodge-podge: coffee, tulip, common rue, basil, monkshood, daffodil, betony. So he made an alphabetical index, minutely written, on the back of his class schedule, which he folded and kept inside the notebook.

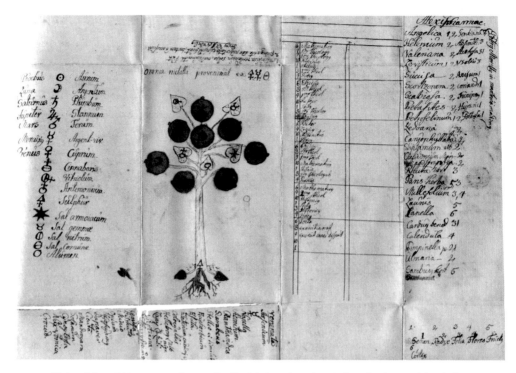

This side of the page from Carl's high school notebook shows his daily class schedule (right of center), a list of alchemy symbols (far left), and the rest of the notebook's index continued from the other side.

When the notebook was new, he'd written his formal school name with a flourish on the first page—Carolus N. Linnaeus—plus a few choice quotations from books by various authors:

If there is a single way towards health, it must be tested, even if it is dangerous.

The best medicines in the hands of an ignoramus are like a sword in the hands of a lunatic.

Many have not recovered because of too many remedies.

He copied directions for concocting herbal remedies—how to use lovage and cloudberries to fight scurvy, how to make blue ink from cornflowers and green ink from danewort (this entry he wrote in green ink, which remains green to this day). He included recipes to rid the human body of colic, stones, worms, even frogs.

Southernwood placed inside the pillowcase, he wrote, would get rid of fleas and lice. Parsnip was said to have special protective powers: "Anyone who smears himself with its sap will, without being harmed, be able to pick up a snake." But beneath that he wrote himself a sharp warning: "Do not take the risk. This hot soup is not for me."

Then, of course, there was the pumpkin. *Cucurbita* in Latin, *pumpa* in Swedish. Rub pumpkin leaves all over a horse, he wrote, and mosquitoes or gadflies will not bother it.

Carl was not struggling in all of his classes, just the ones crucial for graduation and his future as a clergyman: theology, ethics, rhetoric, oratory, Greek, and Hebrew. However, in all his academic misery, one bright spot emerged.

The local physician, Dr. Rothman, who had received a medical degree from the University of Harderwijk in Holland, was hired to teach a smattering of botany and medicine to Växjö's crop of future Lutheran clergymen. The boys had to be prepared: in rural communities far from Sweden's few doctors, parishioners desperate for medical help would turn to the best-educated person around—their pastor. These boys had a lot to learn.

Rothman's medical garden demonstrations and field trips served up a smorgasbord of fascinating facts—basil eased heart

In his student notebook, Carl drew a tree rooted in a checkerboard land-scape like the fields, meadows, and woods back home.

palpitations; betony drove thick fluids from the head; black radish restored hair growth; borage reduced melancholy; nasturtium strengthened the memory and sharpened the mind. Carl took it all in, writing in his notebook. The doctor, seeing Carl's enthusiasm, invited him to help in the garden where he grew plants to make ointments, tinctures, and salves to treat his patients.

Carl didn't know how to tell his parents about his failing grades. His father, a poor country pastor, had sacrificed to scrape

Nils Linnaeus and Christina Brodersonia, Carl's parents.

up the money for tuition, and his mother had made her expectations clear: Like it or not, he was to follow his father, grandfather, great-grandfather and uncles into the family business, the church.

Carl didn't want to disappoint his parents; he loved them. He didn't know what he was meant to do, but he was sure life in the clergy wasn't it. He believed in God deeply. But study Latin, Greek, theology, rhetoric? No thanks. Carl was painfully aware that he did not fit in. The natural world had a gravitational pull that he couldn't resist. He wanted to be rambling through fields or slogging along the lake's marshy edge—not kneeling at a bench with the other boys getting his knuckles whacked raw by the Latin master for every wrong answer. His church was the fields, the gardens, the woods. He saw evidence of God in these fascinatingly complex worlds, not in Latin class. He worried that his father wouldn't understand. He knew his mother wouldn't.

So there was bad news and there was worse news. The bad news Carl had known for a while—he was barely making it in high school. The worse news was that his father was destined to find out.

◇◇◇

It happened in September 1726. His father was ill and traveled to Växjö to see the doctor of the province. When he arrived at the village, he headed first to the Cathedral School for a progress report from the headmaster. With Carl only a year away from entering university, Pastor Nils Linnaeus was expecting good news.

The headmaster did not mince words: Don't waste your money, he said. Carl will never be a pastor or a scholar. Take him out of school immediately and apprentice him to a shoemaker or a tailor so he can learn a useful trade and earn a living.

The headmaster's news did not help Nils feel any better.

But the doctor, Johan Rothman, who was also Carl's teacher, disagreed with the headmaster's assessment. He saw a spark in Carl that the other teachers had dismissed as unimportant from their Cathedral School perspective, and urged Nils to consider the medical profession for his son. The doctor felt so strongly about the boy's abilities that he made the father an unbelievable offer: he would tutor Carl in botany and physiology, the study of how living organisms function, for free.

Nils took him up on the offer but, generous as it was, he knew this would not be good news at home. Handing down the parish from father to first son was tradition in Christina's family and other families like hers. The church was a stable ladder to success and security, while medicine was a shaky, low-status profession.

For medical help, people had few options. Surgeons, physicians, and apothecaries had various kinds and amounts of training and skill. If a person needed a rotten tooth pulled or a broken bone set—or a haircut—he'd go to the shop with a red-and-white spiral pole out front, a sign of the trade of blood and bandages. There, the barber-surgeon would apply knife skills learned during his military experience sawing off limbs in battle. He could remove bladder stones, give a shave, or perform bloodletting to balance the body's fluids, or "humors."

A person with a heart, liver, brain, or stomach problem would go to a physician who treated illnesses with medicines, special diets, exercise, and therapeutic baths. A few, like Dr. Rothman, had an actual medical degree. People also called on apothecaries who collected, selected, and prepared medicines for healing. They sought out folk healers. It wasn't easy being sick. It was even harder getting well.

Nils knew that his God-fearing wife, Christina, thought the church was the only acceptable option for their oldest son. She was not alone in looking down on medicine as an occupation. Considering the times, it would be easy to forgive her anxiety,

NOTHING FUNNY ABOUT THE FOUR HUMORS

In the first half of the eighteenth century, medical practice was still based on the theory, proposed by the ancient Greek physician Hippocrates (460–377 BC), that the body had four humors, or fluids: blood, phlegm, yellow bile, and black bile. Blood was hot and moist; phlegm was cold and moist; yellow bile was hot and dry; black bile was cold and dry. These humors were considered to be the basis for people's predominant moods, or temperaments (hence the phrase "being in a good humor" or "a bad humor"): the four temperaments were sanguine (optimistic, upbeat), phlegmatic (cool, unemotional), choleric (angry, hot-headed), or melancholic (sad). In a healthy person, each humor was balanced in the right proportion.

Galen, physician to the Roman emperors around 160 AD, added to the theory, assigning the qualities of hot, cold, moist and dry to diseases and the drugs to cure them.

Many old theories, like this one, persisted unchallenged because the Europeans revered the classical medical writers—Aristotle, Hippocrates, and Galen—and even the best medical schools used their writings as standard texts.

especially if she knew the story of her own great-grandmother. Johanne Pedersdatter was a *klok kone*, a Norwegian term for a "wise woman" who knew how to use plants to heal the sick. The villagers claimed she'd murdered the bishop's wife with black magic—in other words, that she was a witch. Her son, Christina's grandfather, was only ten years old when his mother, who had been tortured into confessing, was burned at the stake in Stavanger, Norway, in 1622.

When Nils returned home, he didn't mention any of Carl's bad news to his wife. Several months later, he worked up the courage, and Christina burst into tears. "Is poor Carl to become nothing but a simple barber surgeon?" she cried.

Devastated, Christina's hopes for a son in the church zeroed in on her second son. Eight-year-old Samuel, who loved plants too, was no longer allowed anywhere near his father's garden.

◇◇◇

In Växjö that fall, Dr. Rothman treated Carl like a son. He began teaching him to approach botany not as a hobby but as serious study. Since Carl preferred personal observation to abstract ideas, they worked to improve his organizational skills and memory by making tables, diagrams, and drawings. Dr. Rothman showed Carl how to organize his notes into rows and columns. These systematic arrangements provided visual memory aids and encouraged Carl to compare and evaluate information from different sources—and also saved expensive paper. Plus, when spread out on a single sheet, gaps, inconsistencies, and patterns all became easier to spot.

More modern, updated science now permeated Carl's notebook. Still, he copied in some classic definitions, as if to prove wrong his mother's skeptical view. One equated a physician who is also a philosopher with God himself. Carl underlined another, Julius Caesar's description of what it takes to be a doctor:

> a man learned, honest, mild, conscientious, mature, happy, who trusts in God, who is not puffed up by his knowledge, his labour or his success, who is not too fond of money.

Carl now knew exactly the future he wanted—"to be medicus and botanicus and nothing else."

When he arrived home for Christmas vacation, Carl entertained his younger siblings by playing doctor to their imaginary wounds and illnesses. There were four of them now, ages sixteen to three—Anna Maria, Sophia Juliana, Samuel, and Emerentia. He took their pulses and, carving lancets out of wood, pretended to "bleed" them to balance their "humors." He thrilled his brother and sisters by brewing up harmless herbal potions for their make-believe ailments. They all felt good . . . until the time came for Carl to return to school.

As spring turned green, so did his room in Växjö. But the more plant specimens he found, the more jumbled his collection became. The more jumbled his collection, the harder it was to track down specimens he knew he had. He couldn't compare and contrast them if he couldn't even find them. He needed to make sense of the chaos.

Dr. Rothman suggested sorting them into groups by their observable similarities. First, though, they had to select a trait to guide the organization. This dilemma had perplexed scientists for centuries. Everyone organized plants differently—some by color, some by shape of various parts, some by habitat, or alphabetically by name, or geographically, or by the plants' medical, agricultural, or household uses.

Carl and his teacher chose the method devised by the celebrated French botanist Joseph Pitton de Tournefort, who had grouped plants into twenty-two "classes" according to the shapes of their flowers—bell, cup, cross, funnel and so on. Those classes

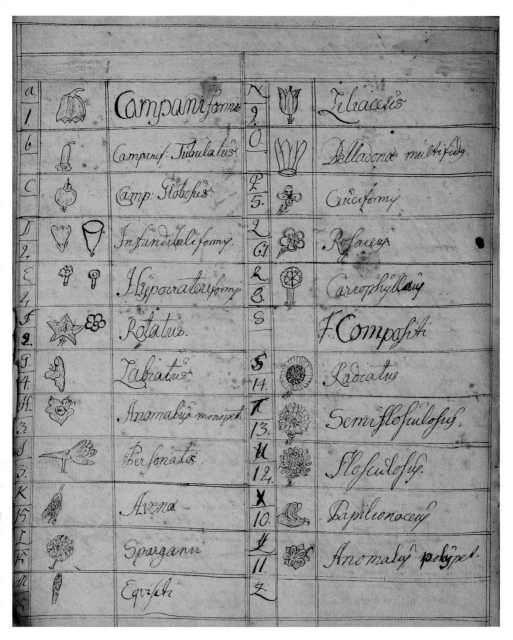

Carl made this copy of Tournefort's chart of classes in his notebook as a guide for organizing his own collection of plant specimens.

were then broken down by their fruits into 698 subgroups. Tournefort chose the Latin word *genus*, meaning "type" or "kind," to refer to each subgroup; the plural is *genera*. Each plant was placed first in a broad class and then in a more specific genus.

That spring, Dr. Rothman, who tried his best from this remote part of Sweden to follow the news of scientific theories and innovations, wrote a summary in Swedish for Carl of a wildly controversial speech that discussed the structure of flowers. It had been given almost ten years earlier by a student of Tournefort's, a French surgeon named Sébastien Vaillant, and had only recently been translated into Latin, the language in which Dr. Rothman read it.

Tournefort insisted the flower's internal structures were organs that excreted waste, and that the "dust" that fell off flowers was a waste product. This mysterious and hotly debated substance was termed *pollen,* a Latin word which at the time referred to any powder or fine grain. Vaillant disagreed with his teacher. He argued that the parts inside the flower—the stamens and pistils—did not excrete waste. They were reproductive parts. Plants, he said, reproduced sexually. The stamens were male, the pistils were female, and pollen was not waste. It was a "volatile spirit," the "breath" of life that enabled a plant to produce offspring.

That plants might reproduce sexually was not an idea that originated with Vaillant. In 1682, British physician Nehemiah Grew had suggested it. His countryman, botanist John Ray, wrote in support of the theory, citing date palms and spinach

Sébastien Vaillant scandalized Parisians with his lecture on plant reproduction.

as examples. Finally, in 1691, Rudolph Camerarius, a German physician, proved it in an experiment using a plant called dog's mercury (*Mercurialis*), repeating it with spinach and hemp. When Camerarius isolated flowers without "dust" from those with it, the seeds either failed to develop or were infertile.

Many botanists in Europe had come to accept the theory, but not Tournefort. News of Camerarius's important experiment ran in an obscure German publication and never "made headlines."

Other than a handful of botanists, few Parisians had heard of it when Vaillant delivered his memorable "X-rated" lecture at 6 a.m. on June 10, 1717, in the King's Garden in Paris to a crowd of six hundred. In his speech, Vaillant used human reproduction as a colorful metaphor for plant reproduction, referring to the dust grains as "embryos with powdery feet," dust sacs as "testicles," seeds as "true eggs," and the bud as the "nuptial bed."

Some professors were outraged by what they considered a disrespectful attack on their deceased colleague. Tournefort had been killed in an accident in 1708, crushed against a wall by a speeding carriage. Others were shocked by Vaillant's terminology. Such talk was considered crude in polite Parisian society. Better that this sort of discussion be dry as a desert and explained in the dullest possible way. On the other hand, two hundred members of the audience that morning—young medical students—applauded enthusiastically.

◇◇◇

At his school in Sweden, Carl pored over Dr. Rothman's handwritten summary, engrossed.

Even if Carl sensed, after reading Vaillant's speech, that this was a big idea, he didn't yet know what to do with this new understanding. What questions he pondered, at nineteen, are lost to history. Did he make a connection with the evidence he'd seen himself, the pumpkin plant in his father's garden that failed to produce pumpkins? Did he realize then that this theory explained the mystery, since the male flowers—the ones with pollen—had been snapped off before the pollen could reach the female flowers to fertilize the pumpkins? Did he wonder which trait would be most essential for a plant—that its flowers were yellow, white, or blue; or that its flowers were shaped like a bell, a funnel, or a cup; or that its leaves were oblong, triangular, or lobed, or . . . the way in which it made more plants?

Whatever his questions were then, one answer would become clear to Carl Linnaeus over time: in the natural world, the most important trait was a plant's ability to sustain life by making more plants. This key understanding would eventually guide all of his life's work.

For now, Carl put Vaillant's idea aside and went back to his immediate task—organizing his unruly plant collection. But this seed of an idea germinated and grew. Flowers, he was beginning to see, were all about sex.

◇◇

EVERY GROWING THING

Minerals grow; *Plants* grow and live;
Animals grow, live, and have feeling.

—CARL LINNAEUS, *SYSTEMA NATURAE*
(THE SYSTEM OF NATURE), 1735

Grain fields and marshes fringed the slow-moving water outside the city walls. Inside, the ribbon of river bisected the small city of Uppsala, Sweden. On one bank sat shops and houses; on the other, the medieval red brick cathedral towered over the university. Here, as in the famous Latin Quarter along the river Seine in Paris, neighbors and passersby could overhear students speaking in Latin, the universal language of scholars. Among those young scholars was twenty-one-year-old Carl Linnaeus, from the low rolling hills of southern Sweden. After graduating from Växjö, at age twenty, and spending a year at Lund University, he transferred to Uppsala in the fall of 1728 with one purpose: to learn all he could about the natural world.

Uppsala University, founded in 1477, was Scandinavia's

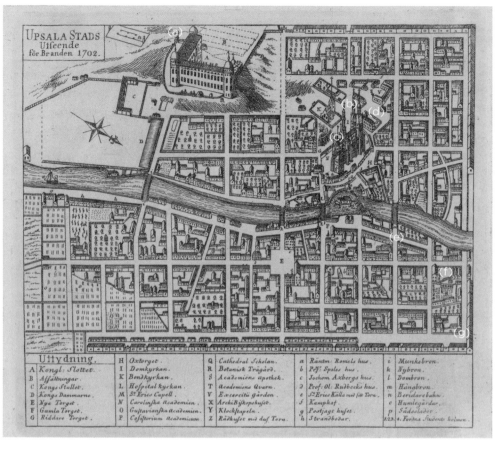

A 1702 map of the walled city of Uppsala and the river that ran through it. Included are the king's palace (a), the cathedral (b), the university hospital (c) and anatomical theater (d), Dean Celsius's house (e), Dr. Rudbeck's home (f), and the medical gardens (g).

first university and the alma mater of Linnaeus's teacher. Dr. Rothman assumed the school was still as he'd experienced twenty years earlier and had convinced the young man that he would find botany courses there.

What Linnaeus found, however, were just two talented but

disheartened medical professors, Olof Rudbeck the Younger and Lars Roberg. Nearing seventy, Dr. Rudbeck the Younger, professor of anatomy, botany, zoology, and pharmacology, was no longer young. In a massive fire that had ravaged the city in 1702, he had lost most of his unpublished twelve-volume work about his expedition into Lapland (today called Sápmi), as well as thousands of illustrations prepared for another lengthy book. Since the fire, he had spent most of his time in pursuit of a new interest—comparing the Sami and Hebrew languages. He spent little time teaching. The anatomical theater, which had been built in 1662 by his father, Olof Rudbeck the Elder, was rarely used now.

The other professor, Dr. Roberg, taught theoretical and prac-tical medicine, surgery, physiology, and chemistry. He'd fought to keep open his poorly funded teaching hospital (Sweden's first), even renting out one room as a tavern. When the hospital was forced to close, Dr. Roberg turned to tutoring private students and seldom gave public lectures. It was no wonder that of the five hundred students at the university, only ten were studying medicine.

With just one hundred silver coins—all his parents could spare—Linnaeus enrolled in school, paid rent, and bought food. To afford a few of Roberg's costly private lectures on Aristotle and his course on medicine, he skipped meals. In January, four months after he arrived in Uppsala, the last of his money went to a month-long stay in Stockholm to attend an autopsy with six lectures at a professional physicians' organization. Four hundred miles from home and in debt, he had to borrow money for food and line his worn-out shoes with layers of paper to keep out the snow. These hungry winter months imprinted on him a lifelong anxiety over money.

Learning alone, self-directed and without regular classes, Linnaeus worked hard on projects of his own, occasionally asking Rudbeck and Roberg for advice. He frequented the university's library where he savored a century-old work—sheets holding three thousand dried European plant specimens bound into twenty-five large books. He joined his "student nation," one of the regional groups of students similar to today's fraternities. Yet nowhere among his fellow students could he find a like mind to spur him on.

Classmates told him that the university's most brilliant medical student had gone home to care for his dying father. When the student, Peter Artedi, returned to campus in March, Linnaeus rushed to meet him.

"We immediately started talking about stones, plants, and animals," Linnaeus recalled. He was amazed both by his new friend's knowledge and his willingness to share it.

Two years older, tall and thin with long black hair, Artedi reminded Linnaeus of a picture he'd seen of the English botanist John Ray. In contrast, Linnaeus was short and sturdy with reddish brown hair. Linnaeus described his friend as determined and modest, a man of integrity and honor, someone who took his time forming opinions, while he described himself as spontaneous, passionate, and intense, someone who made friends easily and did everything in a hurry.

They couldn't have been more different. Or more the same.

As Linnaeus's parents had, Artedi's parents pushed their son to become a clergyman like his father and grandfather.

Their son, too, disappointed them by choosing medicine. In their schools, both boys had learned Aristotle's ideas from the same texts that boys in ancient Rome might have read. Artedi had already made a list of the plants in his home province. Another of his interests was alchemy, chemistry's medieval forerunner, which held that matter could be transformed. Alchemists experimented, for example, to find ways to turn common metals, such as lead, into precious metals, such as gold. Artedi lived quietly on the outskirts of Uppsala where he tutored a potter's children and used the potter's kiln for alchemical experiments.

Peter Artedi also investigated zoology, especially fish. This fascination began at age eleven when his family moved to a northern area on the Gulf of Bothnia, whose tributaries were known for salmon-spawning runs.

The two met daily. When one made a thrilling discovery—a new mushroom, a new bird, a new idea—he'd try to keep it to himself. After a few days, though, he would be bursting to share his news with his best friend. Each was the other's sounding board. The friendly rivals worked independently but also compared notes. Fierce competition energized their ideas.

◇◇◇

Across the river from the university, behind the botany professor's official residence, a small swampy garden backed up to a creek. Neglected since the great fire, the once lush medical garden was now a sorry tangle of weeds. Where 1,500 species had grown, only a few rare plants poked through the couple hundred surviving species.

One April day as Linnaeus rummaged through the weeds, a clergyman strolling in the garden asked about some plants. He rattled off the names he'd learned from Tournefort's book. On further questioning, he retrieved his herbarium—a book he'd created of more than six hundred native wildflowers he'd collected, pressed, glued onto paper, and bound together. The clergyman, it turned out, was Olof Celsius, theology professor, dean of the cathedral, amateur botanist, and the owner of a well-known garden that Linnaeus had been longing to see.

While professors occasionally took in students as paid boarders, Dean Celsius was so impressed with this raggedly dressed student that, soon after, he offered meals at his table, a rent-free room, and access to his private library.

Months later, Linnaeus had a chance to thank him formally. It was tradition at New Year's for Uppsala students to write flattering poems for their favorite professors. Instead, Linnaeus wrote an essay, "Prelude on the Wedding of Plants," for his benefactor, Professor Celsius:

> I am no poet, but something, however, of a botanist; I therefore offer to you this fruit from the little crop that God has granted me. . . . In these few pages I treat of the great analogy which is to be found between plants and animals, in that they both increase their families in the same way. I beg you graciously to accept this humble gift . . .

Linnaeus's essay elaborated on the main points of Sébastien Vaillant's Paris lecture and borrowed the Frenchman's colorful, provocative style to describe how a flowering plant reproduces

Linnaeus gave this handwritten essay to his benefactor, Professor Celsius, as a New Year's gift in 1729. The drawings show pollen transfers between dog's mercury plants of different genders (left) and pumpkin flowers of two genders with pollen floating between them (lower right). He wrote the title in Latin, "Preliminaries on the marriage of plants in which the physiology of them is explained, sex shown, method of generation disclosed, and the true analogy of plants with animals, concluded."

through pollination. In an eyebrow-raising comparison with human sexual reproduction, he wrote that pollination is the plant's sexual act, comparing pollen to sperm, seeds to eggs.

Despite the startling metaphor, the ideas in the essay intrigued Celsius. He shared it with his colleague Dr. Rudbeck, the botany professor. When Linnaeus applied for a job working in the university's medical garden that spring, Dr. Rudbeck rejected his application. Instead, he offered him a far more important position: that of botanical demonstrator—showing students how to identify particular plants and use them in treating patients' symptoms. This job was normally performed by the professor himself or a senior-level student, but on May 4, 1730, Linnaeus, a second-year, largely self-taught student, delivered his first garden demonstration. Not once had he heard a lecture on botany at Uppsala—his reason for attending the university. Yet his knowledge was clear and his passion for plants was contagious. From then on, instead of the usual seventy or eighty attending such demonstrations, as many as four hundred students packed into the garden.

When his mother learned that Linnaeus was giving lectures for a professor, she was relieved. At long last her son was redeemed in her eyes. He might have a future after all.

To boost his small income, Linnaeus also began giving private lectures on botany. Many of his students were older than he was, and many were sons of wealthy families and nobility. Some paid cash: twenty-four copper dalers per class. But most paid him in old books and much-needed cast-offs, such as used shoes, shirts, hats, stockings, gloves, buttons, even a toothpick to clean his teeth.

Meanwhile, Dr. Rudbeck, having been married three times and the father of twenty-six children, needed a tutor for his three youngest sons. He asked Linnaeus to move in to tutor them and teach medicine to their older stepbrother.

Living in the Rudbeck household gave Linnaeus priceless access every day to Rudbeck's knowledge and guidance, as well

Uppsala university student, of about the year 1700, elegantly dressed in fancy wig, embroidered waistcoat, cravat, tricornered hat, ceremonial saber, and shoes with heels.

The short-eared owl (*Asio flammeus*) painted by Olof Rudbeck the Younger around 1710.

as time to examine the professor's extensive botanical library, collections, and exquisite bird paintings. He was also able to make improvements to the university gardens outside the professor's house.

Perhaps best of all were evenings when the professor would tell stories of his travels as a young man into the wilds of Sápmi in northern Sweden. Thirty years earlier, Rudbeck had accompanied astronomers on an expedition to the Arctic Circle. His tales inspired in Linnaeus a longing to see the rare northern plants and animals for himself.

◇◇◇

About a year before moving in with the Rudbecks, Linnaeus had begun to puzzle out a new way to organize his dried plant collection. He decided to produce a small catalog of the rare plants he'd found, to test the three most popular systems against one another:

> In France, Tournefort had organized plants by flower shape;
>
> In Germany, Augustus Rivinus used the petals;
>
> In England, John Ray used the fruits, flowers, seeds and roots.

Linnaeus compared them as he classified specimens from his collection and showed his results in a handwritten paper, "Spolia Botanica." Always fond of military metaphors, he called these results *spolia*, meaning "spoils," as if he'd plundered them from the war between those feuding systems. Like the reuse of old building stone for new construction, he was drawing on the three existing systems to see if something new and better could result.

He concluded that the Englishman Ray's organizing system, which compared the flowers, seeds, fruit, and roots of different plants to determine relationships among them, was the most natural. A natural classification system, the ideal as Linnaeus saw it, was one based on relationships between plants as God had made them. However, Ray's method had so many criteria to evaluate that it was hard to use. When confronted with an unknown plant, beginning plant-hunters, like Linnaeus's students, would be swamped by the number of details they had to find, such as the number of tiny developing leaves inside the seed.

Tournefort, on the other hand, went to the opposite extreme—from too many to too few. His system had only one simple criterion—the shape of the flower. That made it easy to use but produced many strange and unnatural groupings. Like any system based on an arbitrary selection of criteria, such as flower color or, in Tournefort's case, flower shape, Linnaeus considered it artificial because it was a human choice. It was like grouping people into families by their eye color or height instead of by their relationships. In addition, he disliked that Tournefort separated trees from other plants.

He also ruled out Rivinus's system. Even though it classified trees and other plants together, the scheme was based on the number and similarity of petals. Since not every type of plant had petals, he judged this system to be artificial as well.

Linnaeus believed that the most natural system for grouping plants would center on the reproductive parts (the fruit and seeds), instead of the vegetative parts (the leaves, stem, and roots) which support and protect the fruit and seeds. In a truly natural group, he believed, related plants might have similar properties. Such a system would be more than merely a means for scientists to identify and describe plants. It might also help in finding substitutes for expensive foreign imports such as tea, coffee, spices or medicines—plants with similar properties that could be grown locally. Science needed one consistent, universal system that everyone could use.

◇◇◇

Meanwhile, in the university's garden, Linnaeus's students struggled to take notes during his information-packed demonstrations. They asked for help. To eliminate "the great inconvenience of copying all names with pen flying, in the Garden under the open sky, which after all seldom can be done without errors," he listed all the plants around Uppsala in a handwritten guide. In it, he tried out his new organizing system for the first time.

Peter Artedi also was frustrated with the existing systems, especially when it came to umbellate plants, such as Queen Anne's lace, parsnip, parsley, fennel, dill, and water hemlock. Like umbrellas, they held up their many tiny flowers on stalks of nearly equal length. They fascinated him. Artedi began plotting out a new way to classify these plants.

During their several years at Uppsala, Carl Linnaeus and Peter Artedi worked so closely that it is sometimes hard to tell where the ideas of one ended and the other's began. They both had been examining animals and minerals as well as plants. So it was a logical next step for the two to tackle one of the eighteenth century's most pressing natural science challenges: the organization of nature. Plants, animals, minerals . . . everything.

An encyclopedia of life.

This was a pivotal decision. Needing to break the monumental task into manageable chunks, they first assessed their individual passions, strengths, and weaknesses. Then they carved up the three kingdoms.

Artedi took fish, amphibians, and reptiles.

Linnaeus took birds and insects.

Both worked on minerals and the four-footed creatures called quadrupeds.

Artedi took the umbellate plants, and Linnaeus dealt with all the others.

As they made their selections, these two forward-thinking friends were motivated not only by scientific ideals and a sense of mission, but also by their need to make a living. Their choices clearly aligned them with the interests—and possibly even the jobs—of their aging mentors: Linnaeus with Rudbeck, Artedi with Roberg.

They realized that they needed to examine animals, plants, and minerals from around the world to do this work. But they also understood a reality of their time—that travel was dangerous. So the two friends swore a pact: if either died before they finished their joint task, "the other would regard it as sacred duty to give to the world what observations might be left behind by him who was gone."

They believed their work was that important.

3

◇◇◇

INTO THE ARCTIC!

Mountains upon mountains rose before me in every
direction . . . I now beheld the Lapland alps.
—CARL LINNAEUS'S JOURNAL, 1732

The day before his twenty-fifth birthday in May 1732, Carl
Linnaeus saddled a horse. With the spring semester behind
him, and having secured Artedi's promise in case he didn't
return, he was looking for adventure. Captivated by Professor
Rudbeck's stories and thrilled by the possibility of finding rare
northern species for his big project, he set his sights on a place
the Swedes called Lapland.

Lapland straddles the Arctic Circle, an imaginary line that
rings the globe far north of the Equator. Inside is the top of
the world.

This frozen frontier seemed a mysterious, dangerous, even
frightening place to Europeans. Fed by rumors and travelers'
tales, they believed it was inhabited by trolls, witches, and
hostile worshippers of pagan gods. The people who lived in this
wild country were called Lapps. A common theory is that this

was an old Finnish term meaning "people who live apart from others." Today their descendants are called by their own term, the Sami people, pronounced "sah-mee." They call their region Sápmi. These nomadic reindeer-herders, hunters, and fishermen have lived in this glacial wilderness for thousands of years, but in Linnaeus's time the region remained largely unknown to outsiders.

Funded by a small grant from the Royal Society of Arts and Sciences, Linnaeus's mission was twofold. First, identify plants, minerals, and animals that could be used as foods, medicines, building materials, paints, or dyes. Second, study the lifestyle and health of the Sami people. He wanted to find out how they lived in such a cold climate, what they ate in times of scarcity, and how they used plants. From the Samis, he hoped to learn different ways of using naturally-occurring materials that could benefit the rest of the country.

Linnaeus packed two maps of the northern region, plus a journal with an inkhorn and goose quills, several unfinished manuscripts, paper for pressing plants, a spyglass, a magnifying glass, and an eight-sided measuring stick. He brought clothes for his five-month expedition—one shirt, two pairs of detachable half-sleeves, two nightcaps, a comb, and a hat with netting to protect against mosquitoes. He wore leather trousers bought secondhand at an auction, and a tied-back wig. He carried a short sword, a pistol for shooting birds and other small animals for his specimen collection, and, in his pocket, a passport and a three-by-five-inch field notebook. Its pages had been specially treated by rubbing chalk on the surface until the paper was smooth, hard, and could be wiped clean with water. While traveling, Linnaeus penciled hasty notes into the notebook. At the end of each day, he inked the notes into his permanent journal, then wiped the notebook's pages.

Alone and riding a hired horse, Linnaeus pushed the pace and covered forty-three miles on the first day. Over the next weeks, he mounted and dismounted, examining trees, smaller plants, and dew-sprinkled "mathematical webs" of spiders. He noted mineral springs, quicksand by the coast, and, along the road, chunks of "spar full of talc, or Muscovy glass, glittering in the sun." He noted changes in soil and rock types and various kinds of plants and animals.

On the coast, Linnaeus visited Swedish and Finnish settlers. Never passing up a chance to talk with local people, he peppered them with questions. This young man, who collected insects from cattle and later from reindeer up north, and asked countless odd questions, must have seemed strange. Occasionally he thought their answers were preposterous. Anthropologists have observed that sometimes local people, bored by endless questioning, have fun making up outrageous stories to tell wide-eyed visiting scholars. That might have been the case in one village where locals tried to fool him with an old folktale. They explained to Linnaeus that "malignant beings of gigantic size" had hurled rocks to try to knock down their church. Nearby, a boulder held their evidence: imprints of four enormous fingers and a thumb. In his journal, he wrote down their story and described these villagers as naive peasants. But in another village, Linnaeus sympathized with a woman whose stomach was making croaking noises. She was convinced that she had swallowed water containing frog eggs and could feel three grown frogs jumping inside her. He'd heard of this complaint before and suggested ingesting tar to induce vomiting, but she had already tried that without success. Elsewhere, people told him about an old woman who stole an apple from a tree and angered the owner. The old woman cursed the tree and it never grew apples again. Linnaeus was suspicious and the next morning went to inspect the tree. It was an elm. Since the locals did not recognize the elm, he concluded that this was the edge of that species' range. Linnaeus's observation showed that determining what is "not" an apple tree can be as valuable to science as learning what "is" an elm.

Traveling north toward the Arctic was like time-traveling. The seasonal clock ticked backward from spring into winter. Snow replaced spring flowers. Days lengthened, and the midnight sun lit his way. He rarely saw stars. One night, awakened by bright light streaming in the window, he jumped out of bed, worried there was a fire. The sky was ablaze with a natural light show— the aurora borealis.

Travelers along this road could stop at an inn every twelve miles or so for a drink or a meal, to hire a fresh horse or to leave a letter to be picked up by a post-rider. Linnaeus sent home a heavy package of rocks that he had collected. In the evenings, he transferred his day's notes with a quill pen and ink into his permanent trip journal and added details as he remembered them. Overnight guests bunked together, several to a bed where hungry fleas hopped from guest to guest. The post-houses, he complained, were "dreadfully bad."

However, when Linnaeus left the coast road for the wilderness, he missed those inns—their beds, their bread, their fresh horses. He also missed people who could speak his language. Since Linnaeus spoke only Swedish and Latin, he hired interpreters and guides. Some nights in the back country he slept outside, and others he spent at the homes of local officials or clergymen.

Fallen trees crisscrossed the path like a game of giant pick-up-sticks. Storm-soaked birch branches drenched him. His horse, spooked by two reindeer, tried to buck him off. Farther along, the horse stumbled over roots and rocks. It fell through a rotten bridge into a creek. Its owner could afford to equip it only with a rope tied around its jaw and an unstuffed saddle. Riding it left Linnaeus saddle-sore and exhausted.

To make matters worse, at the village where he thought he'd meet Sami people trading with coastal settlers, the annual spring market had already ended. To interview the Sami, he would have to find their summer fishing camps. There was only one way to get through that deep wilderness. By water.

◇◇◇

A man agreed to take him partway up the Ume River. His "sewn boat" was constructed in the traditional Sami way with spruce planks overlapped and stitched together using cord "as thick as a goosequill," according to Linnaeus's description. The hull's ribs were made from spruce roots, and two boards cut from branches of the same tree spanned the boat crosswise for seats.

As they moved upriver, the calm water soon turned white as it rushed toward the sea from its source in the Scandinavian Moun-

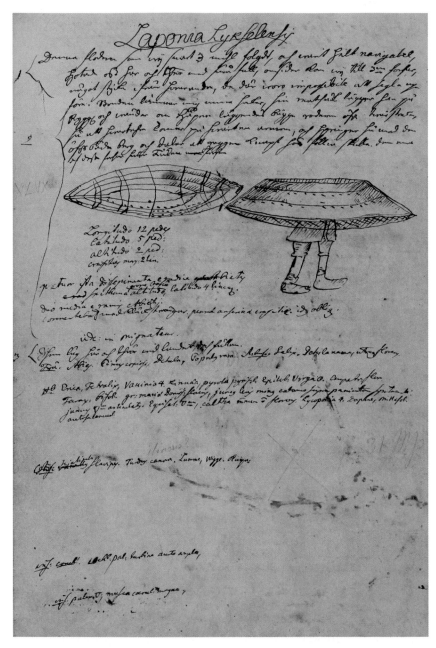

A page from Linnaeus's Arctic journal, showing a Sami "sewn boat." It measured twelve feet long, five feet wide, and two feet deep. Linnaeus's drawing of his guide portaging the boat is not to scale.

tains. Linnaeus and his guide portaged around rapids. Linnaeus carried the gear, while the guide stowed the oars and hefted the twelve-foot-long wooden boat, bottom up, onto his shoulders. Linnaeus followed the man who "scampered away over hills and valleys, so that the devil himself could not have [kept] up with him." In other unnavigable stretches, they trudged through the frigid water, towing the heavy boat.

One morning, after traveling all night, they rested at a dismal place called Lucky Marsh. They dumped icy water from their boots, built a fire, and hung their clothes on bushes to dry. The guide hiked ahead to look for someone familiar with the area who could replace him. Meanwhile, Linnaeus tried to sleep. The north wind chilled him on one side, the fire scorched the other, and gnats bit without mercy.

The next afternoon, the guide returned with an elderly Sami woman. Her skin was stained and leathery. When she spoke, the woman surprised him by speaking in an old, formal Swedish. She explained that there was no one available to guide him further and advised him to turn back. She had little to give but offered a fish. Its mouth was crawling with maggots. Instead of accepting the fish, Linnaeus talked her into selling him one of the three reindeer cheeses she had stored in a hut a mile away. Heading back downriver with his guide, he grumbled that the place should be renamed Unlucky Marsh.

It was early June. Frost and snow still clung to the riverbanks. Jagged rocks lurked beneath the water's surface. Maneuvering around rocks and downed trees, the guide struggled to control the boat in the forceful current. It was a rough ride.

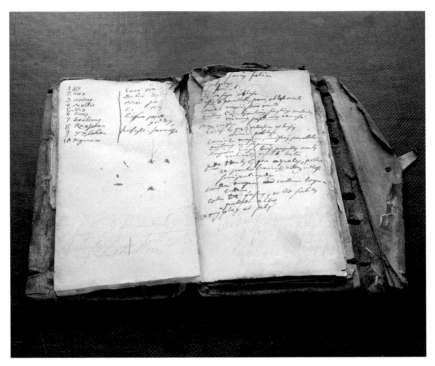

Linnaeus's field notebook from his Sápmi expedition.

Despite the guide's skill, the boat crashed into a boulder and collapsed, flipping the men into frigid, waist-deep water. As they fought their way to shore, they scrambled to save their belongings. Lost to the river were the man's shattered boat, hatchet, and several pike he'd caught. Linnaeus lost two birds—a large black heron and a red-colored jay—that he had carefully preserved for his collection. Amazingly, his journal survived the plunge.

After the two hiked from the crash site back down the river, Linnaeus continued walking along the coast alone. When he reached the Lule River, he hired another boat and guide in a second attempt to strike deeper into the wilderness. Finally, five weeks after leaving Uppsala, he crossed the Arctic Circle near the village of Jokkmokk.

◇◇◇

Seeing the Scandinavian Mountains for the first time left Linnaeus awestruck. This was epic beauty. Having grown up in the flatlands, he thought they looked like "a range of white clouds rising from the horizon." He estimated that these rugged, snow-covered "alps" were, in places, more than a Swedish mile high (equivalent to more than six modern miles or about 10 kilometers), which would have made them taller than Mount Everest. Linnaeus carried no equipment to measure heights or even distances, and his estimates were extreme. In fact, Kebnakaise, the tallest mountain in Sweden, is only 6,909 feet.

While the peaks were far lower than Linnaeus guessed, they were still too steep and hazardous to climb in icy conditions. So he never saw the high alpine plants that grew there. However even at lower elevations and in the valleys, he found so many new plants that he wondered how he would deal with them all.

> When I reached this mountain, I seemed entering on a new world; and when I had ascended it, I scarcely knew whether I was in Asia or Africa, the soil, situation, and every one of the plants, being equally strange to me . . . All the rare plants . . . were here as in miniature.

He discovered one hundred plants in Sápmi that had never been described before.

Crossing fields of packed snow in the Scandinavian Moun-

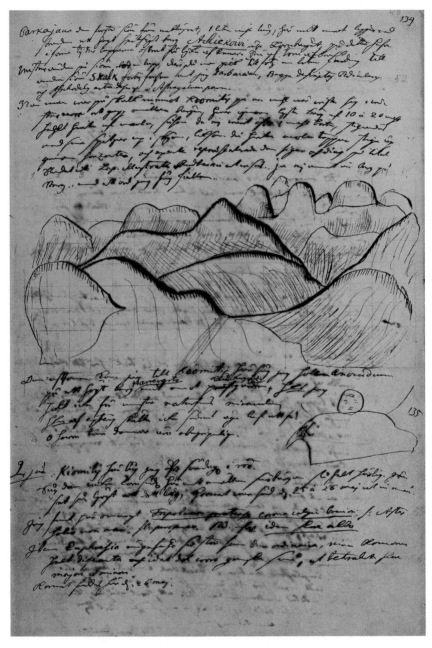

Linnaeus's sketch of the rounded tops of the Scandinavian Mountains. "The lofty mountains, piled one upon another, showed no signs of volcanic fire."

tains, Linnaeus's footing became unsure. Sometimes the snow held firm, sometimes it crumbled like loose sand. Rivers of meltwater flowed below, undermining the snowpack. At one place, he took a step onto deep snow and the surface crust of ice suddenly gave way. He sank in, trapped. His guides, an old Sami father and son, quickly rigged rescue ropes and hauled the soggy young scientist to safety. The next day, Linnaeus and his guides rose early and hiked to a "lofty icy mountain . . . of a very great elevation, and covered with perpetual snow." There they crossed a glacier, a river of ice hundreds of feet deep. Crevasses in the glacier revealed strata which had formed as each new snowy layer rested on the layer from the year before and compressed the snow below into ice.

Rain chased by a cold east wind froze their clothes to an icy crust. The wind blew them along, knocking them off their feet. Linnaeus rolled downhill to a stop—at the edge of a crevasse.

The mountain chain they crossed curved like a backbone down the Scandinavian peninsula. After hiking for miles across ice, snow, and bald, stony mountains, they reached a place where the watersheds divided. Linnaeus observed that the surface waters now flowed westward. Eventually the party caught a view of the Norwegian Sea. Ahead lay Norway's coast with forests, fjords, islands, meadows of wild clover, and a few small cottages. Linnaeus looked forward to drinking cow's milk again and sitting in a chair. On a warm hillside, he slumped down, exhausted, by a patch of his favorite food—wild strawberries—and ate.

Meanwhile, his guides, seventy and fifty years old, who had carried all of his gear, were full of energy, sprinting up and down the slope. A friend of Linnaeus's, Dr. Nils Rosén, had asked him to try to find out why the Sami were such fast runners. Did they position their feet differently when running? How did they have such stamina?

Linnaeus credited several reasons. Unlike the high, heavy-heeled shoes worn by European men, the Samis' shoes had no heels. This natural foot position allowed them to run as easily as though they were barefoot. They developed stamina from lifelong daily exercise chasing reindeer.

Another factor contributing to the Samis' agility and their good health, he thought, was their diet. He noted that "In spring they eat fish, in winter nothing but meat, in summer milk and its various preparations." He believed their habit of eating food cold was healthy too. "They always let their boiled meat cool before they taste it, and do not seize it . . . as soon as it comes out of the pot." They ate small amounts of food at a time, unlike Finlanders who "cram themselves with . . . turnips" and Swedes who gobbled flummery, a sweet dessert.

Linnaeus ate foods prepared by his guides and hosts. In addition to reindeer, the Sami people ate wild birds, fish, squirrel, marten, bear, and beaver. During the winter months, when the fish they'd preserved was no longer edible, a family of four ate at least one reindeer a week until they could start fishing again in the spring. The Sami men prepared all the meat, fish, and birds. Linnaeus praised their rare consumption of alcoholic beverages. As a high-energy treat in that cold climate, they offered guests a spoon of grease.

The women milked reindeer and made cheese. Sometimes the

Samis traded with the Swedish and Finnish settlers who grew grains. Linnaeus was fascinated to discover that when flour was scarce during times of famine, the Samis ground the less edible parts of grains, called chaff, and the inner bark of pine trees which they baked into loaves, like bread.

At times, local customs took him by surprise. For instance, when visiting a guide's relative, the guide and his family member touched noses, a greeting he had never seen before. At another Sami cottage, the family's dishwashing procedure robbed him of his appetite. The host spat into Linnaeus's spoon and dried it with his hand, while his wife cleaned the bowl, licking her fingers after every swipe.

Outside his hosts' huts, Linnaeus slept between reindeer skins, sometimes sheltered by an overturned boat. The Samis cut their beds out of mattress-sized pieces of moss. These soft beds could be rolled up and carried. When the mattress

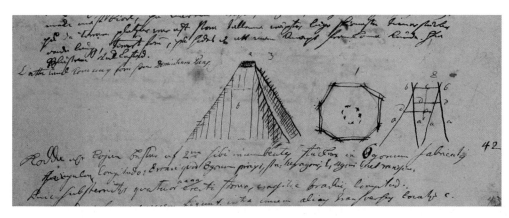

A wooden Sami hut, sketched by Linnaeus. This permanent dwelling of the Forest Sami was typically 11 feet high by 12 feet wide. A hole at the top vented the open fire pit directly below.

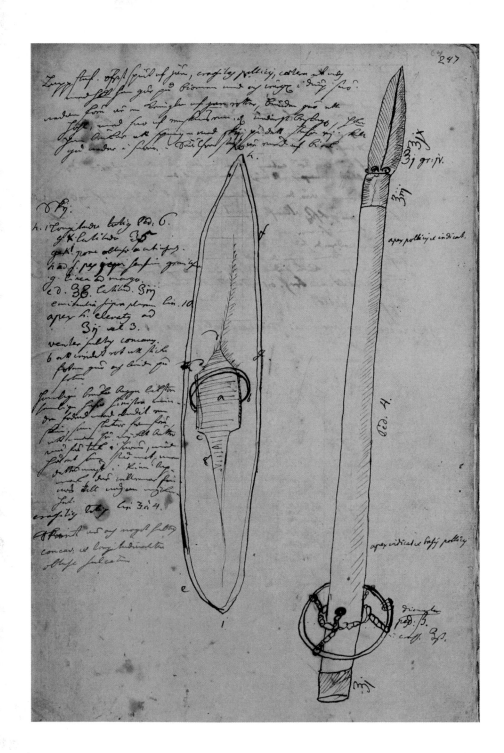

dried out and flattened, a sprinkle of water puffed it back up like a sponge.

Overall, Linnaeus considered the Samis' self-sufficient life-style, free of coffee, sugar, and salt, as the ideal, and contrasted it with what he considered the pampered ways of his fellow Swedes. He attributed the Samis' good health to their diet and the pure mountain air and water. Their hardiness, he concluded, was due to the constant exposure to cold temperatures that their herding lifestyle required.

◇◇◇

Linnaeus criticized the treatment of the Samis by the Swedish state church, which required them to attend religious festivals and fined them if they failed to appear. No matter the season, they had to brave dangerous rivers and travel great distances, and often arrived, as he commented, "half dead with cold and fatigue." In his trip journal, he also pointed out other injustices, such as heavy taxes imposed by the government even while foreign fishermen were allowed to encroach on the Samis' tradi-tional fishing grounds.

At times he showed great sympathy for the Samis. Yet at

OPPOSITE: Linnaeus's diagram of a six-foot-long wooden ski. Skis did not exist in southern Sweden at the time. Partly covered in reindeer skin to prevent the wearer's foot from slipping, the ski was tied to the ankle with a twist of fir root. The Samis used only one ski pole. At the base of the pole, a six-inch loop of reindeer leather kept it from sinking in the snow. The iron spear on its upward end was used to attack bears or wolves in deep snow.

other times, his journal entries sound patronizing and condescending. For example, he recorded the names of some clergymen and government officials who offered him lodging and tours of their gardens, but he never identified by name any of the Sami people who helped him along the way. He wrote about them not as individuals with personalities and things to say, but by their functions—rower, porter, host, or guide.

What impressed Linnaeus most about the Samis was their understanding and careful use of their region's natural resources. They sewed colorful, ornately embroidered clothing from reindeer hides. To make thread, Sami women used their teeth to separate the leg sinews from the fresh carcass of a reindeer into fine strings which they twisted together. He brought back a sample that he claimed was superior to the finest Swedish thread.

To clean the floor, a Sami woman tied a brush of spruce fir twigs to her right foot and swept her way around the room. To join wood for a hunting bow, Samis made glue by boiling down perch skins. From birch bark, they fashioned plates, boat bailers, shoes, baskets, and tubs in which they salted fish. They made birch-bark collars to keep rain from trickling down their necks.

If they needed to find their way in the woods, they turned to nature's compasses. More branches grew on the south side of large pines than the north; bark was rough on the north side of aspen trees but smooth on the south; lichens grew on the north side of old, withered pines; and ants built their hills on the south side of whortleberry bushes.

As a future medical doctor, Linnaeus paid particular attention to how the Samis dealt with injuries and illnesses. To treat a blister, they applied a cushion of lichen. To treat a scrape or cut, they made a powder of white bog-moss to seal the wound. For a headache, toothache, or backache, they lit a pea-sized bit of fungus from a birch tree right on the place of pain. The flame, he observed, created an open sore that lasted for months and left scars. He did not mention whether it cured the original pain.

The long cold winters prevented bathing which, of course, led to body odor. Linnaeus noted that a Sami boy wanting to impress a girl would tuck a chunk of fragrant corky fungus from a willow tree into his pocket.

> [I]n other regions [Love] must be treated with coffee and chocolate, preserves and sweetmeats, wines and dainties, jewels and pearls, gold and silver, silks and cosmetics, balls and assemblies, music and theatrical exhibitions: here [it is] satisfied with a little withered fungus!

Linnaeus also described the leisure-time activities and games of the Samis and their children. The children built small stone huts to play in. They used branches from dwarf birch trees as antlers while they pretended to be reindeer fighting one another. Adults carved wooden tokens to play a Sami version of an ancient Viking board game, Hnefatafl (nef-ah-tah-fel), also known as Tafl. Linnaeus called it "tablut," which means table or board game. In this war strategy game with unequal opposing sides, the Swedish king and his eight defenders are surrounded and

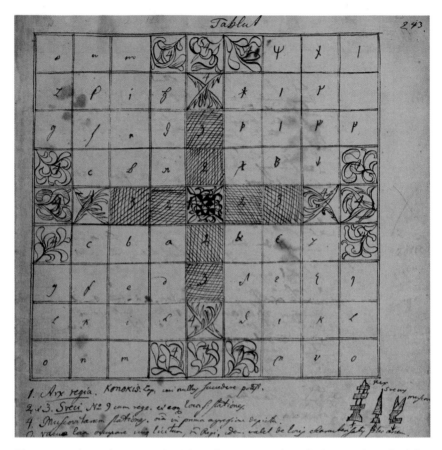

The game board was embroidered on a reindeer hide, easily rolled for storage and transport. Tokens (lower right) were carved from wood. Linnaeus's notes have been used recently to resurrect this 1,600-year-old game.

outnumbered as they try to fight off a force of sixteen Muscovite invaders. Linnaeus recorded the rules in his notebook while watching people play.

◇◇◇

When Linnaeus returned to the university in mid-October, he submitted his report to the Royal Society of Arts and Sciences.

He had been traveling for five months. He had taken three trips inland by way of the rivers Ume, Lule, and Torne. His return trip took him along the Gulf of Bothnia and the Baltic Sea down the coast of Finland. Although he had traveled a long way—2,000 miles (3,200 kilometers)—he more than doubled that distance in his report, to 4,500 miles. Perhaps the inflated number was caused by an unintentional miscalculation, but he was expecting the Society to pay him by the mile.

He brought back an extensive collection of minerals, plants, and animals from the Arctic and, for years, he and his students would draw on them as study specimens, comparing them with similar species from other parts of the globe.

His journal provided material for papers and lectures on many Arctic subjects, including plants and animals, insects, mosses, reindeer, and—a subject very important to him—diet and the Sami lifestyle. Even though he stayed only a few nights with several Sami families in their camps and did not live among them for long periods, as modern anthropologists would, some consider his journal to be a valuable early study of an indigenous people. He wrote of the reindeer-herding life of the Mountain Samis and detailed the daily life of the Forest Samis, nomadic fishing families.

Today Samis lead modern lives with iPads and internet, electricity, cars, and snowmobiles. They live in rural areas as well as cities and towns throughout northern Norway, Sweden, Finland, and Russia. Half the population is bilingual and still speaks one of the Sami languages at home, passing this knowledge on to their children. Under their ancient claims, they

continue to hunt and fish. While fishing is very important to the Samis, few make their entire living from it. The so-called Forest Samis herd reindeer in the lower areas; the Mountain Samis move with their reindeer herds in annual migrations to the mountains along the Norwegian border in summer and back to the coniferous forests in winter.

Linnaeus would use his experiences as a resource in teaching future scientific adventurers: how to collect specimens, how to study a group of people and their way of life, how to explore an unfamiliar land, and how to tell nature's facts from folktales.

Around Uppsala, he also showed off his unusual Sami costume: reindeer-fur mittens, boots without heels, and, strangely, a woman's red summer hat jauntily tipped. From his belt dangled a runic calendar, pouches, and a round snuffbox carved from reindeer horn. No Sami man would ever have worn those bizarrely mismatched items together. Later, a collector from England gave him a Sami ceremonial drum. Early missionaries had burned such drums, with their mystical, shamanic symbols; in the eighteenth century, Swedish law made it illegal for a Sami to own one. Linnaeus played the drum and performed an imitation of traditional Sami nature-based

OPPOSITE: Linnaeus posed for a portrait in his Sami costume while living in Holland in 1737. In his right mitten he holds his favorite Arctic flower, named *Linnaea* in his honor by a friend. Linnaeus later gave the tiny twin-belled flower a two-word name, *Linnaea borealis*. He described it as "lowly, insignificant, disregarded, flowering but for a brief space—from Linnaeus who resembles it." Painting by Martin Hoffman, 1737.

oral poetry called *juoigat*, by the North Samis, but *jojk* by the Swedes (pronounced "yoik").*

◇◇◇

In the fall of 1734, after six years at Uppsala University and his Arctic adventure, Linnaeus was ready to seek his medical degree. There is no evidence that he ever received an academic degree from Uppsala University. Since Sweden had no medical school, most who wanted a medical degree attended schools in Holland. Especially popular was the University of Harderwijk, known for its speedy diplomas.

Peter Artedi had left Uppsala in early September, planning to study natural history in London first, then to enroll in a Dutch medical school. In November, Linnaeus passed the examination on Swedish religious doctrine required for a passport.

Meanwhile, with Christmas approaching, he accepted an invitation, for the second year in a row, to enjoy the holidays with school friends in Falun, a mining village in the province of Dalarna. The season was a swirl of festivities, and at one party, he met and fell for Sara Lisa Moraea, the eighteen-year-old daughter of a wealthy doctor.

Knowing she had many eligible suitors, Linnaeus wasted no time in taking the next step and donning that amazing Sami outfit. On January 2, all dressed up in reindeer skin, fur mittens, and red hat, he called on Sara Lisa and her family for

---

* *Jojk* is included in the opening song in the movie *Frozen,* "Eatnemen Vuelie" (Song of the earth), performed by a Norwegian musician of Sami descent.

the first time. The next day he visited again and found Sara Lisa by herself. Without the customary presence of a chaperone, they had time to talk in private. He penciled into his almanac "absentibus parentibus," Latin for "home alone." Another day, he "called on S. L. M. and had a little fun." On January 20, after frequent visits, he "explicitly solicited" Dr. Moraeus for his daughter's hand in marriage.

Linnaeus had charmed Sara Lisa. She said yes. However, her parents weren't so quick to agree. The reply came a week later. Linnaeus could marry their daughter, but there was a stipulation: he would have to get a medical degree and establish himself as a doctor first; he had three years to do it.

Before he left, Linnaeus gave Sara Lisa a ring and a poem he'd written for her:

A Lover's Farewell

Oh mighty Lord God
a wailing sound
my soul cries
who must leave and say goodbye
to the one who is mine
who my whole heart has in mind
. . .

Moraea my friend
Linnaeus is your servant
who greets you good day
and wishes you pleasure and delight
until he again
may return and see his sweetest friend.

4

<hr/>

DRAGON WITH SEVEN HEADS

Many people said it was the only one of its kind in the world and thanked God that it had not multiplied.

—THEODOR M. FRIES, 1923

The mayor of Hamburg, Germany, was thrilled to show off his prized possession, the famous Seven-Headed Hydra. The taxidermied dragon, looted by the Swedish army from a church altar during the 1648 Battle of Prague, was for sale and was expected to bring a handsome price. The mayor had already turned down a large offer from the King of Denmark.

When Carl Linnaeus arrived in Hamburg in April 1735, he was stunned by the splendor of the city, in sharp contrast with his poor rural homeland. This was his first trip abroad, and the first time he'd walked around a major foreign port. Most of all, he was excited by the opportunity to inspect the unique specimen. He had seen the hydra's image in all its snarling viciousness in the first volume of a natural history thesaurus published the

The famous seven-headed hydra of Hamburg, a flying lizard, and two American birds, pictured in Albertus Seba's *Thesaurus*.

year before by Amsterdam's renowned apothecary, Albertus Seba, a big-time collector of curiosities.

The editor of a respected journal, the *Hamburg Reporter of New Things Learned*, had been corresponding with Linnaeus. The enterprising young Swede, who was a genius at self-promotion and far from modest, had sent the editor several letters that glowingly described his scientific travels through

Sweden, curiosities he had collected, and manuscripts he would be bringing to Germany and Holland in hopes of finding a publisher. Scholars believe he may have written these letters in the third person, like articles, similar to today's press release style. "All this skilful man thinks and writes is methodical . . . His diligence, patience, and industriousness are extraordinary." The editor now offered to escort Linnaeus to view the monster.

There it was: seven heads, seven gaping jaws, countless needle-sharp teeth. The seven heads seemed evidence enough to Linnaeus that the creature must be a fraud. Up close, he saw that the threatening teeth and two clawed feet had once belonged to weasels. The body was covered in snake skins carefully glued together.

Linnaeus figured that imaginative Catholic monks in Prague had created this semblance of the "dragon in the apocalypse" to frighten their parishioners into goodness. When Linnaeus told people he met of his unveiling of the hoax, word got out and the dragon was worthless. Claiming to be worried that the mayor would seek revenge on him for his part in devaluing the treasure, Linnaeus hopped on the next ship to Holland.

◇◇◇

An important goal of science has always been to separate fact from fiction. As seventeenth- and eighteenth-century explorers brought back curiosities from their travels, people began to collect them. In England, their room-sized collections were called "cabinets of curiosities." In Germany, they were called *wunder-kammer*, or "wonder-rooms."

While wealthy amateurs assembled these collections, scholars in various fields were collecting knowledge of all sorts into books—almanacs, encyclopedias, and word books. In Holland, Seba worked on his natural thesaurus and, in France, Linnaeus's rival, Georges-Louis Leclerc, the comte de Buffon, was compiling an encyclopedia of natural history in forty-three volumes. But between nature and the supernatural, the lines were sometimes

The Danish physician Ole Worm built this cabinet of curiosities in the 1600s. The word *cabinet* referred to a room, not a piece of furniture. Some collectors' wonder-rooms contained sculptures and paintings. Others held fossils, bones, horns, and taxidermied animals, as well as spears and other human artifacts from various cultures.

blurred. Scholars still tangled with persistent superstitions, talk of witches and black magic, old-fashioned medical theories, worrisome tales of dragons, and folk stories that often misinterpreted nature.

For example, two years before Linnaeus stared down the seven-headed dragon, he faced another confused bit of folklore. During his 1732 expedition to the land of the Samis, he met a back-country preacher and a schoolmaster who told him that clouds were solid objects that struck the Arctic mountaintops and carried away rocks, trees, and animals including cattle, reindeer, and vole-like rodents called lemmings. Linnaeus argued that clouds could not lift anything; clouds, he explained, were "watery bubbles" that floated up into the air. The two men remained unconvinced. Too much knowledge, they scoffed, had muddled the young man's brain.

To be fair to the preacher and schoolmaster, Linnaeus had some blind spots, too. He suggested that a wind had carried these things away, and later attributed the Sami cloud myth to men and animals stumbling and falling to their deaths down mountain crevasses. Today we know that a pair of lemmings can give birth to as many as one hundred young every six months and that overpopulation quickly results. When that happens, hordes of lemmings "mysteriously" disappear—in search of food elsewhere.

Despite many pioneering observations, Linnaeus was not thoroughly modern. For instance, he never stopped believing that swallows overwintered in the mud at the bottom of lakes.

He was not alone in his naive ideas: one seventeenth-century naturalist believed swallows wintered on the moon.

In the eighteenth century, educated people struggled to separate nature's facts from folktales and the wild accounts of travelers. Imagine what it was like to analyze vivid reports of ridiculous-looking things. A bird with rodent's teeth and leathery wings that slept hanging from the roof of a cave. A fish that could fly. A plant that ate insects. An animal that hopped on two giant feet and kept its babies in a pocket. Or an ocean phenomenon called the Maelstrom—a giant whirlpool that swallowed ships.

The famous seven-headed hydra of Hamburg became Linnaeus's test case for what to believe. As he worked on cataloging the natural world, he weighed what was possible and what was absurd, listing the animals that he knew to be real. Any that were suspicious he placed in a separate category called "Paradoxa," meaning absurd or unbelievable. He described common explanations for these puzzling creatures. His intent was to debunk the fantasy creatures and demystify science.

At the top of the list of Paradoxa, of course, was the seven-headed hydra. Next came the South American "frog-fish," a frog which supposedly transformed into a fish. Linnaeus dismissed this because frogs breathe through lungs, not gills, and fish have gills, not lungs. This creature was impossible according to the rules of nature, he said.

Then he listed the monoceros, or unicorn. It had a horse's body, the feet of a beast of prey, and a long, spiralling horn. "A painter's invention," he wrote, although the monodon, or narwhal, had a similar horn. Linnaeus's friend Peter Artedi had seen a specimen of the tusklike tooth and confirmed the existence of this sea animal. Narwhal horns were mislabeled as unicorn horns in many curiosity cabinets.

Also on Linnaeus's list of impossible creatures was the satyr. This one was said to have a beard, a tail, and a hairy, manlike body—"if ever one has been seen," Linnaeus remarked. He determined that it must have been a species of monkey.

Another creature, *pelecanus*, was a bird with a preposterous neck pouch hanging from its gullet. Medieval authors claimed this bird pecked its own flesh for blood to feed its young. Linnaeus decided that this absurd-looking creature was another product of imaginations run amok. He later realized that he had guessed wrong, and that the pelican was indeed a real bird.

The Scythian lamb also made this list. In the Middle Ages, people said that this plant, also called the Vegetable Lamb of Tartary, contained blood and looked like a lamb, even attracting animals of prey. Linnaeus determined it was actually a tree fern with woolly horizontal roots that lay, like fuzzy lambs, on the ground.

Many authors had written about the phoenix. It was said to be the only bird of its species in existence. Linnaeus summarized its fantastic story: "After having been burned to death on the funeral pile, which it had itself constructed out of [aromatic plants], it revived in order to live the happy period of youth." He figured this was not a bird but a date palm tree which, when burned to the ground, would rise up through the ashes and grow again.

Then there was the goose-barnacle. People who had never seen geese breeding in coastal European habitats believed that these barnacles "nested" on coastal tree branches and then fell into the ocean where they gave birth to geese. Linnaeus explained that barnacles were actually shelled sea creatures which attached themselves to driftwood floating near shore. Their feathery appendages filtered the incoming tide for food. Barnacles hatched barnacles, and geese had geese for parents.

On quiet summer nights, people stared at their ceilings and worried about the tick-tick-ticking of the deathwatch beetle in the rafters and walls. They thought this creature kept vigil over someone about to die. While Linnaeus did believe in ghosts and omens, he attributed the ticking to the fact that the beetle burrowed in wood. We now know that the beetle makes this sound by bumping its head against the wood. Why does it do that? To attract a mate. Later, its larvae hungrily bore tunnels through the rafters.

◇◇◇

Despite the occasional deathwatch beetle, homes were people's safe havens. Beyond their villages, a scary world of unknowns lay in wait. Oceans upon oceans ended who knew where. Their watery depths contained who knew what.

Norwegian sailors, American whalers, and seamen from every country returned from years-long voyages with bone-chilling stories of sea monsters that swallowed boats whole. The Norwegians called them *kraken*. They said that a single kraken with its long tentacles could take down a sailing vessel and all souls

Published in Buffon's encyclopedia, this drawing of a "kraken octopus" by French naturalist Pierre Denys de Montfort was inspired by a 26-foot-long tentacle found in the mouth of a sperm whale in 1783.

on board. The reports probably described giant squid, which we now know can be nearly sixty feet long and weigh two thousand pounds. Linnaeus eventually classified this real animal as a cephalopod, a member of the same group as octopus, squid, and cuttlefish.

Other animals that Linnaeus added to his list of questionable creatures included:

Antilope, a deerlike animal with twirled horns (it was real);

Lamia, a Greek demon that sucked the blood of children (not real);

Manticore, or man-eater, with a lion's body, human head, three rows of sharklike teeth, and a tail that could shoot poisonous spines (not real);

Last was the siren, which was part-bird, part-woman. This creature's song was said to cause shipwrecks by luring sailors toward dangerous rocks. Strangely, Linnaeus was unsure about this one. Both he and his friend Peter Artedi seriously considered the existence of sirens and mermaids. Eventually Linnaeus, who had never seen one either dead or alive, speculated that the reports were mistaken sightings of manatees, dolphins, or seals.

Linnaeus eventually dropped the category "Paradoxa," perhaps assuming that he had put an end to the false myths.

Owners of curiosity cabinets also began to turn their focus away from fabulous impostors toward real plants and animals. Wealthy collectors now wanted their collections to be scientifically authentic. Some hired trained naturalists to improve their collections and to create accurate labels and catalogs. Over the years, Linnaeus would be hired to slay fake "dragons" and organize the shells, flowers, minerals, and animals in many extensive collections, including those of the Swedish king and queen.

◇◇◇

After his abrupt departure from Germany, Linnaeus arrived in Holland at the University of Harderwijk, armed with a brief thesis on malaria. He had written it back in Uppsala, where people often contracted and sometimes died from this fever when Uppsala's humid summer weather descended along the swampy river Fyris. In the thesis, he incorrectly blamed the sickness on particles of clay in drinking water. Scientists would not know until the end of the nineteenth century that the real cause was a parasite spread through mosquito bites. However, Linnaeus apparently presented a convincing argument. He defended his thesis before the faculty at the Dutch university and on June 24, 1735, six days after arriving, he received his medical degree.

Now open for business, Linnaeus found both his botanical and medical services in demand in Holland.

5

<><><><><><><><><><><><><><><><><><><><><><><><><><><><><><><><><><><><><>

CAN BANANAS
GROW
IN HOLLAND?

Dawn was always a friend of the muses.

—CARL LINNAEUS, LETTER TO JOHANNES BURMAN, JANUARY 1736

As a young, new doctor in June 1735, Carl Linnaeus was short on money but loaded with ambition. He traveled from Harderwijk to Amsterdam, a city of leisure and elegance, of silk clothes and foods with foreign tastes and strange aromas imported from distant places. Crucially, to Linnaeus, the city was a hub of scientific activity. He rushed around introducing himself to leading scientists and hustling his revolutionary ideas about how to reorganize the natural world. Ever since he and Peter Artedi had divided up the task of classifying the natural world during their student days at Uppsala, Linnaeus had been steadily organizing and refining his system. By the time he arrived in Amsterdam, he was ready to publish his ideas—but first, he needed a job.

Linnaeus had a strong personality and sky-high self-confidence and often left a bad first impression. Despite this, most people were won over by his intelligence and irrepressible charm on meeting him a second time. Now with medical degree in hand, he was in a hurry to launch his career and return to Sweden to marry Sara Lisa.

In Amsterdam, Linnaeus found he could trade his botanical expertise for a room and meals with Johannes Burman, director of the city's botanical garden.

Twenty miles away, Burman's friend George Clifford lived in luxury on his country estate, Hartekamp. Clifford was enormously wealthy. Heir to a banking dynasty, he was a director of a powerful commercial empire, the Dutch East India Company. This century-old business had a trading monopoly on imports from the lands around the Indian Ocean. Clifford, a botanical collector, could get anything he wanted from anywhere in the world. His sea captains kept the gardeners on his estate busy unpacking crates of exotic plants and animals.

One day, Clifford invited Burman and his Swedish house-guest to tour his magnificent estate. The garden was a living catalog of nature's diversity. Only a privileged few had ever seen it. The estate was like "paradise," according to Linnaeus. The private zoo was alive with wildness—the roaring, growling, grunting, and howling of tigers, monkeys, antelopes, and wart-hogs. In the aviary, Linnaeus spotted pheasants, American falcons, teals, sandpipers, swans, coots, buntings, African grey parrots, crossbills—so many birds, he said, that the garden echoed and re-echoed with their calls.

As they walked the shaded paths and man-made hills, they

passed statues and mazes, topiary shrubs carved and snipped into artistic shapes. Flowerbeds splashed color everywhere.

Then they came to four buildings with large windows. These greenhouses were called orangeries by the French because they protected citrus trees and other cold-sensitive plants from freezing in the northern climate.

In the first grew southern European plants; in the second, Asian plants; in the third, African plants; and in the fourth, strange species from the New World. Some Linnaeus had read about, but most he'd never seen. What he saw in that last greenhouse hypnotized him.

Enormous green bladelike leaves reached for the ceiling, stretching high above New World magnolias, sassafras, cacti, and orchids. No flowers, no fruit; the plant was all leaves, wrapping tightly around each other at their base, fusing together to form a column that looked like a tree trunk. From the column's center, new leaves rose and unfurled.

Even though the plant had no fruit, he knew immediately that it was a banana plant. In Europe, only royalty and the richest citizens had ever seen a banana, let alone tasted one. They called it a *pisang*, a word borrowed from a Javanese language.

Linnaeus wondered whether Clifford's tropical plant could actually bear bananas in Holland. Only three gardens in Europe—one in Austria and two in Germany—had ever managed to produce the fruit. Dutch gardeners, famous for their skill and the highly profitable tulip trade, had never produced a banana. Even the famous botanist Antoine de Jussieu had tried at the royal garden in Paris and failed.

Engraving of the banana plant made in 1736, from a painting by Dutch artist Martin Hoffman. The height of Clifford's banana plant is not known, but most stand between 12 and 40 feet tall.

Odds were that the specimen in Clifford's greenhouse would not do any better. Still, the challenge excited Linnaeus. This could be a dramatic test of his botanical mastery, a way to prove himself. In addition, since affluent Europeans craved expensive imports like tea, coffee, silk, spices, and cacao for chocolate, he wondered whether those imports could be grown in Europe. Perhaps this greenhouse, with its banana plant, would be a good place to start investigating the question.

Clifford was impressed by Linnaeus and offered him a job. For a thousand guilders a year, plus free room and board and access to Clifford's carriage and extensive contacts, he would serve as the wealthy man's live-in physician. At fifty, Clifford was worried about his health. Like a hothouse plant, he would require constant care. More compelling to Linnaeus, though, was that in this position he would also curate the gardens, supervise the greenhouses, and reorganize the herbarium, Clifford's collection of dried specimens.

There was one problem: Linnaeus had already promised to help Burman prepare a book on plants. The thought of losing his botanical adviser upset Burman. Luckily, in Clifford's library, Burman spotted a rare book that he'd never seen before—volume two of Sir Hans Sloane's *A Voyage to the Islands of Madera, Barbadoes, Nieves, St. Christopher's and Jamaica.* Clifford owned two copies and suggested a swap. Linnaeus was traded for a book!

A month later, on September 13, 1735, the young doctor moved in. Promising to stay the winter, he remained for more than two years. With his usual abundance of enthusiasm, he

MEASURING TEMPERATURE

During the first half of the eighteenth century, many people were experimenting with thermometers. Most put a drop of mercury, a liquid metal, into a reservoir at the bottom of a glass tube. As the mercury got warmer, it expanded and rose higher in the tube. Thus, temperature was measured in relation to a fixed point. Some people used the local temperature for this fixed point—a hot summer day in London, or a cold cellar deep under a Paris observatory—or used the temperature of melting ice mixed with salt. One even used the blood of a dying ox. As a result, there were around thirty different scales to choose from.

Among the experimenters was Linnaeus's friend and colleague Anders Celsius. A nephew of Linnaeus's mentor in Uppsala, Olof Celsius, he was a physicist and the professor of astronomy in charge of Uppsala's new observatory. Over two years, Celsius made remarkably precise measurements of water temperatures taking into account the influence of atmospheric pressure. He chose the points at which water boiled and started to freeze as the fixed points on his temperature scale. Unlike the

began to describe all the plants at Hartekamp and worked for a month with Georg Dionysus Ehret, an extraordinary botanical artist who made paintings of the plants. He also dug into the greenhouse work with Clifford's talented German-born gardener, Dietrich Nietzel.

The banana plant had been brought from somewhere in the Americas five years earlier. Since then it had "passed a miserable life," said Linnaeus, "without any amorous incentive."

A banana plant is monoecious, meaning it has both male flowers to produce pollen and female flowers to bear fruit on the same plant. So far, Clifford's plant had produced neither hot London day and the cold Paris cellar, instrument makers in other parts of the world could replicate these two fixed points. However, Celsius's thermometer was confusing visually. He put 0° (boiling) at the top and 100° (freezing) at the bottom, so it had increasing numbers for decreasing temperatures. That was awkward, a little like looking at the world while standing on your head.

Although it is not known what kind of thermometer Linnaeus used in Clifford's hothouse, in 1743 (seven years later) he placed an order for a Celsius thermometer for the Uppsala garden, and asked Sweden's top instrument maker, Daniel Ekström, for an easy modification—to flip the numbers. Now 100° was marked at the top, for water's boiling point, and 0° at the bottom, for its freezing point—the way it is today. When the Uppsala greenhouse got hotter, the mercury rose and the number of degrees increased. When the greenhouse got colder, the mercury dropped into the danger zone heading toward 0°. This made it more intuitive and easier to understand. Linnaeus and Ekström weren't the only ones making this simple change. Instrument makers in France and Switzerland also turned Celsius's scale upside down.

◇◇

flowers nor fruit. Did it lack something from its natural habitat? Maybe the soil, or the amount of water, wasn't right. What would happen, Clifford asked his experts, if you could simulate the hot, humid conditions of the tropics, where bananas grow vigorously?

Linnaeus took up the suggestion. First, he and Nietzel needed to be able to measure temperature in the greenhouse. Back then, few people owned a thermometer. This meteorological instrument cost as much as a musket or a blacksmith's wages for an entire month. Fortunately, cost was no problem for Mr. Clifford. So armed with the high-priced gauge, Linnaeus and

Nietzel boosted the greenhouse's temperature and humidity to mimic the tropics. Next, they repotted the plant in rich soil. They withheld water for a few weeks and then, to imitate a monsoon-like tropical downpour, they deluged the plant with water. They waited and watched.

About four months after their work began, on nearly the first day of the new year, the banana plant showed signs of change: From the center of its trunklike stem, a stalk called a peduncle pushed upward. At the tip, six whorls of maroon bud-shaped bracts appeared.

On January 24, the first bract opened. Like purple awnings over a window, the outer covering lifted and revealed a row of small, pale yellow flowers underneath.

Come early, Linnaeus urged in a letter scribbled hastily and delivered to his friend Burman. Come at dawn—no later than noon—to see our flower at its best. The next day, carriages began rolling up to Hartekamp with naturalists who wanted to see this extraordinary plant for themselves. Burman rushed out with friends—a lawyer, a merchant, and a professor from Amsterdam. Even the most important medical professor of the day, Dr. Herman Boerhaave—a man so famous that a letter from China reached him addressed only to "a Monsieur Boerhaave, Europa"—made the trip.

Over the next several days, the showy purple bracts opened one at a time outward from the peduncle, displaying many rows of small, pale flowers. "These flowers did not all grow fully on the same day," Linnaeus wrote, "but succeeded one another step by step, day by day, with different qualities and differing natures."

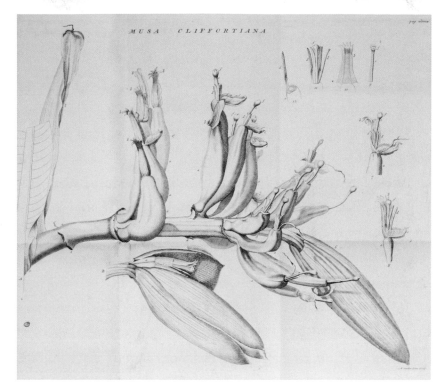

This illustration of Clifford's banana plant from Linnaeus's book *Musa Cliffortiana*, shows flowers emerging in groups, one row at a time.

Linnaeus made daily notes of progress. "What is the meaning of honeyed liquid in any flower?" he asked, looking for explanations and parallels. "What is analogous to this in animals? Why is it re-absorbed in flowers wherein more perfect fruit has appeared, and not in others?" Linnaeus dissected a leaf and, using a microscope, discovered many fine vessels, "like spiders' webs, white, parallel and tenacious."

On January 30, the sixth bract opened, unveiling the final flower cluster. To commemorate this dramatic event, Clifford commissioned an artist to create two pen-and-ink drawings. One shows the lofty plant with its eight enormous leaves, in a pot.

The second shows the stalk with flowers rendered life-size and its parts neatly labeled.

Yet three weeks later, there was still no fruit.

Despite that inconvenient detail, Linneaus rushed a manuscript to the printer's shop in Leiden, three hours away. The resulting forty-six-page book, *Musa Cliffortiana* (Clifford's banana), was illustrated with two large fold-out copperplate engravings. Linnaeus divided the text into chapters on the species' natural history, various names used across the world, physical characteristics, and natural habitat. He described human uses of the plant—its leaves for roofing material, clothing, umbrellas, and napkins; its fruit for making bread, drinks, medicines, and food. He even included recipes from an Indian kitchen. The book's focus on a single plant was an unusual format—a study of one species. Now this model is called a monograph and used routinely for papers on specialized topics.

In his chapter on natural history, Linnaeus described what he believed were the origins of this kind of plant in the warmest regions of Africa and Asia. He explained that it had later been transported to the Canary Islands, off the West African coast, and in 1516 to Santo Domingo in the Caribbean as a plantation crop. Today, however, scientists trace the origins of banana plants to Malaysia and to New Guinea in Oceania, where people cultivated it around 5000 BC.

In the chapter on names, Linnaeus explained that *Musa*, the scientific name then in use, was a Latinized adaptation of *moaz*, the vernacular Arabic name for the fruit. He believed that a scientific name should either honor a scientist or be taken from ancient Latin or Greek, and he worried that since the Muse was "a goddess of the ancients" some of his colleagues might take offense at a name that could be seen as honoring a pagan deity. He proposed that the name was instead a tribute to Antonius Musa, a physician of ancient Rome. But despite the convoluted reasoning, Linnaeus always enjoyed thinking of the plant as his great inspiration, his muse, and often played with the name's double meaning in his writing.

In the book's final chapter, he explained that some of his contemporaries believed the banana was the unnamed forbidden fruit in the biblical story of Paradise, while others were convinced the fruit came from an apple tree, a mandrake, a fig tree, or even a huge grapevine. Linnaeus declined to weigh in on the debate, on the grounds that it was not relevant to a scientific discussion. Nonetheless, over a decade later, in 1753, he finally chose a scientific name for the banana—*Musa paradisiaca*. The name, which means "the banana of Paradise," suggested where he really stood on the issue.

On March 24, the plant stopped flowering. Still no banana. But at the base of each flower, a lime-green bulge—the flower's fruit-making ovary—had been swelling and elongating. As the bulges grew longer, they looked like fingers pushing their flowers upward farther and farther away from the stalk.

On June 3, the flower petals began to wither and fall away. Now the green fingers looked like a giant's hand. The hand began to yellow.

At last, on July 3, there came success—ripe bananas!

"The pulp was very sweet," said Linnaeus of his first taste, "like glue bubbling with particles of honey." He compared it with the taste of a fig or roasted apples with sugar and cream. This was a happy man.

He was surprised, however, that the fruit contained no seeds. Fortunately, several months earlier, on the day the first flower appeared, a shoot had pushed up from the soil next to the base of the plant. This, Linnaeus realized, meant that the plant was preparing for the next generation. It did not need seeds to reproduce. It had another way—roots and shoots. In plants like this one, a horizontal underground stem, called a rhizome, sends up shoots to grow a new plant.

Although wild bananas are stuffed with big, inedible seeds, the fruits of the plant that Linnaeus and Nietzel cared for in Clifford's greenhouse had no visible seeds. Botanists now know that forms with smaller seeds were selected for cultivation by native peoples from banana plants that had varied naturally because of hybridization and mutation in the wild as well as during their cultivation. The seeds had become tiny, infertile specks, while rhizomes perpetuated those varieties.

For eight days, the fruits ripened on the plant. Then black spots began to freckle the skins, and the bananas did what bananas do: rot, rot, rot.

It had been an extraordinary experience for Linnaeus, and he was disappointed when the plant withered and died back.

Linnaeus had built his reputation on his Sápmi journey. His job in Holland launched him on the global stage. And the banana plant, his muse, catapulted him into his future.

6

◇◇◇

NATURE'S BLUEPRINT

We count the number of species as the number of different forms that were created in the beginning.

—CARL LINNAEUS, PRINCIPLE NO. 157, *PHILOSOPHIA BOTANICA* (THE SCIENCE OF BOTANY), 1751

Two months before Linnaeus began work at George Clifford's estate, a familiar lanky figure in black had surprised him at a tavern one morning in Leiden. It was July 8, 1735. Almost a year had passed since his best friend, Peter Artedi, had left Sweden to study abroad for his medical degree. Now there he stood in the tavern, newly arrived in Holland.

Dutch taverns were popular places. A person could buy a mug of coffee or steaming hot chocolate or a tankard of ale, eat a meal, hear a lecture, read newspapers, debate current events, and even pick up mail. They were also places where old friends could bump into each other.

Artedi had been in London, where he met with British scholars and studied private natural history collections, including those of Sir Hans Sloane, whose collections were so extensive that they later became the foundation for what is today the Natural History Museum. Artedi was eager to talk about his latest observations and his new classification system of fishes. He probably described a "Greenland whale" that he'd seen in London the previous November. It had two blowholes on top of its head in front of its eyes. Linnaeus discussed the project he was working on with a printer there in Leiden—a chart-style overview of nature's three kingdoms, which as students the two friends had dreamt of mapping.

His money nearly gone, Artedi faced the unhappy prospect of returning home to Sweden without a medical degree. A companion of Linnaeus's helped out by supplying him with three of his own extra shirts, and Linnaeus told Artedi about an opportunity. For more than thirty-five years, in his apothecary shop by Amsterdam's busy harbor, the rich pharmacist Albertus Seba had bought medicinal plants in bulk and natural curiosities from returning captains and sailors. Having amassed an impressive curiosity cabinet, he was now assembling a three-volume thesaurus of those and other rare objects. Linnaeus knew the first volume well: it included the notorious seven-headed hydra of Hamburg. But Seba, at seventy, was having trouble mustering the energy to finish the third volume, which was, coincidentally, devoted entirely to fishes. Who better than Artedi to provide help? Linnaeus escorted his friend to Amsterdam, and Seba hired him on the spot.

The two friends were so busy working during the next weeks that they rarely saw each other. Linnaeus observed that Artedi was living "a lonely life, went to the tavern from 3 to 9, was at work from 9 to 3 in the night, and slept from 3 till noon."

When they met again in early August, Linnaeus showed Artedi a newly finished manuscript, *Fundamenta Botanica* (The foundations of botany). In it, he distilled the science of botany to a list of 365 concise principles, or aphorisms, organized into twelve chapters like the months of a year.

> **1.** All things that are found on the earth go by the names of elements or natural [bodies].
>
> **2.** The NATURAL [bodies] are divided into the three kingdoms of nature: mineral, vegetable [meaning plant], and animal.
>
> **3.** MINERALS have growth. VEGETABLES have growth and life. ANIMALS have growth, life, and feeling.

Each principle built logically on the one before it.

During their meeting, Artedi, whose work for Seba was nearly finished, insisted on reading aloud another entire manuscript. It was a meticulous classification of fishes that included a description of a fish, *Anableps*, with remarkable two-part eyes that could see above and below the surface of the water at the same time. As the two had done in Uppsala, they scrutinized each point and debated their differing opinions.

When this went on for hours, Linnaeus grew too tired to continue, which he remembered later with regret. "He kept me long, too long, unendurably long (which was unlike our usual practice), but had I known that it was to be our last talk together I would have wished it even longer." On the night of September

27, two weeks after Linnaeus moved to Clifford's estate to reorganize those gardens and tend the banana plant, Peter Artedi dined at Seba's house. It was late when the party broke up and he walked back to his rented room. The next day the police determined that the young man from Sweden, still unfamiliar with the streets along Amsterdam's canals, had lost his way in the dark, fallen into a canal, and drowned.

Devastated, Linnaeus traveled to Amsterdam to identify his friend's body. He arranged a modest burial and, with a loan from the generous George Clifford, negotiated the return of Artedi's manuscript from the hard-bargaining landlord. He needed to keep his promise to his closest friend.

Linnaeus continued their work alone.

◇◇◇

Working day and night, Linnaeus wrote, revised, and polished several manuscripts at once. *Nulla dies sine linea*: Never a day without lines. The quotation, attributed to an ancient Greek artist, was Linnaeus's favorite adage. In addition to his own work, he published Peter Artedi's 532-page book on fishes, a stellar work that one day would earn Artedi the title of "father of ichthyology" (the study of fishes).

By studying nature's exquisite diversity, Linnaeus hoped to identify its underlying scheme and use that scheme to develop a classification system that could be used by every scientist everywhere. To do this required two strategies: first, a way to sort all natural things into groups of similar objects, and second, a consistent way to name them.

How was Linnaeus certain that he could find every one of the species in the first place? This Lutheran pastor's son, like most Europeans then, believed that all species had originated at one point in time—during the Creation as described in the Bible. To him, this meant that no new kinds of animals or plants could ever emerge and that the original species would always remain fixed and unchanging.

Since he thought the number of species could never increase, Linnaeus was convinced that it was possible to inventory nature. Later, in 1749, he wrote:

> If according to gross calculation we reckon in the world 20,000 species of vegetables [meaning plants], 3,000 of worms, 12,000 of insects, 200 of amphibious animals, 2,600 of fishes, 2,000 of birds, 200 of quadrupeds; the whole sum of the species of living creatures will amount to 40,000.

Researchers now describe about 15,000 new species every year. Scientists calculate that there are 8.7 million species in the world today, of which only 1.9 million have been named so far. They also know that some go extinct and others emerge. Therefore, the number of different species changes, and so do the species themselves.

However, having grown up in his little corner of Sweden in the early 1700s, Linnaeus began his career with a limited worldview. Without access to herbaria from other countries or knowledge of the world's diverse natural habitats, he had no idea of the enormity of the project he set for himself.

Much later, with more experience and information, he realized that he had been wrong and that his calculations were way off. His increasing knowledge would eventually inspire him to take a fresh look at the so-called unchanging "fixity of species" and then to question that traditional view. In the meantime, he and his contemporaries still operated under the old notion that no new species could ever come into existence. As he laid out his charts and systems in Holland, Linnaeus felt confident that he could catalog all the world's plants, minerals, and animals.

It may have been a good thing that he started with the limited plants of his childhood home. If he'd also seen all the tropical plants early on, he might have been overwhelmed. That could have kept him from seeing the simple patterns that he needed to create his system.

◇◇◇

Scientists disagreed with one another on how best to order the natural world. They organized their specimens differently. They used different definitions for scientific terms. Occasionally, when duplicate specimens of a species reached scientists at the same time, each scientist gave that species a different name. Only a shared scientific language could eliminate this confusion. One system. One set of rules. One set of names.

Linnaeus believed that he could revolutionize the worldwide study of plants, animals, and minerals by creating a stable base for scientists to work from. But he still had a problem: the established scientists. Could he, a newcomer in his twenties, convince older scientists to follow his plan? How would he ever be able to talk them all into abandoning their own ways of doing things?

For this task, it turns out, he was perfectly suited. Enthusiastic. Passionate. Persistent. A clear communicator. Obsessive about tiny details, yet capable of seeing the big picture. Confident— though, some said, to the point of being egotistical and arrogant. A workaholic. Plus, there was no denying that he possessed one trait especially helpful in bringing people around: charisma.

Along with his friendly charm and boundless energy, Linnaeus had brought to Holland the rough drafts of several manuscripts he had begun as a student in Sweden. Some he had even carried through Sápmi in his pack so that he could work on them while he traveled. These manuscripts were all cogs in a wheel that would move science into the future. He cranked them out, publishing thirteen works—a total of 2,550 pages—during his three years in Holland, all while he was tending to George Clifford's gardens and banana plant.

In these books, the young upstart got rid of the old, conflicting systems. He dumped many names coined by other scientists. No one's work was immune, not even that of his mentors and friends. He tossed out old rules. In their place, Linnaeus developed clear new rules for sorting organisms into groups and rules for coining consistent scientific names. He proposed new rules for describing species so that each description followed the same format. This way someone who was trying to identify a specimen would know exactly where in the description to find the leaf shape, flower structure, roots, or habitat. He wrote clear definitions of botanical terms, listed 935 genus names for plants, and created three charts showing the structure of the animal, plant, and mineral kingdoms. His methodical, practical, list-loving mind felt right at home in the wild flurry of details.

Linnaeus's way of organizing the natural world so inspired two new friends, Jan Frederik Gronovius, a physician from Leiden, and Isaac Lawson, a Scottish physician working in Holland, that they insisted on paying for printing the three enormous charts.

The charts were published in one slim book, *Systema Naturae* (The system of nature), in 1735. It ran only eleven pages but measured 24 inches tall by 18 inches wide. The book's big, complex tables were a typesetter's nightmare. Even though the typesetting began on June 30, the printing was not finished until December 13.

This book would provide the platform for all of Linnaeus's future work. Over the next thirty years, he would revise it a dozen times to keep up with newly discovered species sent to him by colonial traders, ocean-going travelers, and eventually his own students. As he and his colleagues learned more about various species, he used future editions to rearrange the groups. After thirty years of additions and changes, the book's original eleven pages had mushroomed to more than two thousand! It is one of the most important books on biology ever written.

His charts divided each of the three kingdoms—animals, plants, and minerals—into ever smaller groups. Like a box within a box within a box, each chart narrowed from kingdom to class to order to genus to species. This hierarchy, which Linnaeus saw as governing nature, neatly paralleled a country's government of kingdom, province, territory, parish, and village. Linnaeus arbitrarily chose the first three categories—kingdom, class, and order—simply because they were easy to sort. But he intended the last two—genus and species—to reflect natural groups as said to be created by God.

Each chart worked as a spreadsheet. Any recently discovered species could be easily popped into its proper place. Always searching nature for patterns and parallels, he applied the same hierarchy to plants, to animals, and to minerals.

With his charts, Linnaeus was cleaning up the cluttered desktop of science. Scientists finally would be able to know exactly what they had in front of them. No more different names for the same thing, less confusion, fewer cases of mistaken identity.

When it came to animals, in this first edition in 1735, he divided them into six classes:

— four-footed animals (Quadrupedia), based on characteristics of their teeth;

— birds by their beaks;

— amphibians, which included snakes, by their cold body and generally naked skin;

— insects by their antennae and wings;

— fish, using Artedi's carefully-described genera, by the shape of their fins; and

— worms, which included a variety of animals such as earthworms, mollusks, crustaceans, sea cucumbers and sea stars.

FOLLOWING SPREAD: Linnaeus's chart of the animal kingdom, as he understood it in 1735. The original chart is 24 inches tall by 18 inches wide.

CAROLI LINNÆI

I. QUADRUPEDIA.

Corpus hirſutum. *Pedes* quatuor. *Feminæ* viviparæ, lactiferæ.

Ordines.	Genera.	Characteres Generum.	Species.
ANTHROPOMORPHA. *Dentes primores* 4. utrinque: vel nulli.	Homo.	Noſce te ipſum.	H { Europæus albeſc. Americanus rubeſc. Aſiaticus fuſcus. Africanus nigr.
	Simia.	ANTERIORES. POSTERIORES. *Digiti* 5. . . . . . 5. Poſteriores anterioribus ſimiles.	Simia cauda carens. Papio. Satyrus. Cercopithecus. Cynocephalus.
	Bradypus.	*Digiti* 3. vel 2. . . 3.	Ai. *Ignavus.* Tardigradus.
FERÆ. *Dentes primores* 6. utrinque: *intermedii* longiores: *omnes* acuti. *Pedes* multifidi, unguiculati.	Urſus.	*Digiti* 5. . . . . 5. Scandens. *Mammæ* 4. (Ald.) *Calcaneis* inſiſtit. *Pollex* extus poſitus.	Urſus. Coati *Mrg.* Wickhead *Angl.*
	Leo.	*Digiti* 5. . . . . 4. Scandens. *Mammæ* 2. ventrales. *Lingua* aculeata.	Leo.
	Tigris.	*Digiti* 5. . . . . 4. Scandens. *Mammæ* 4 umbilicales. *Lingua* aculeata.	Tigris. Panthera.
	Felis.	*Digiti* 5. . . . . 4 Scandens. *Mammæ* 8. ſc. 4. pect. 4. abdom. *Lingua* aculeata.	Felis. Catus. Lynx.
	Muſtela.	*Digiti* 5. . . . . . 5. Scandens. *Dentes* molares 4. utrinque.	Martes. Zibellina. Viverra. Muſtela. Putorius
	Didelphis.	*Digiti* 5. . . . . 5. *Mammæ* 8. intra burſulam abdomin.	Philander. *Poſſum.*
	Lutra.	*Digiti* 5. . . . . 5. Palmipes.	Lutra.
	Odobænus.	*Digiti* 5. . . . . 5. Palmipes. *Dentes* intermedii ſuperiores longiſſ.	Roſſ. *Morſus.*
	Phoca.	*Digiti* 5. . . . . 5. Palmipes. *Mammæ* duæ umbilicales.	Canis marinus.
	Hyæna.	*Digiti* 4. . . . . 4. *Collum* ſuperne jubatum. *Cauda* brevis.	Hyæna *Veter.* *Vivam Londini nuper vidit & deſcripſit* ARTED.
	Canis.	*Digiti* 5. . . . . 4. *Mammæ* 10. ſc. 4. pect. 6. abdom.	Canis. Lupus. Squilachi. Vulpes.
	Meles.	*Digiti* 5. . . . . 5. *Ungues* medii digitis ipſis longiores. *Corpus* ſuperne albicat: inferne nigricat.	Taxus. Zibetha.
	Talpa.	*Digiti* 5. . . . . 5. *anteriores* maximi.	Talpa.
	Erinaceus.	*Digiti* 5. . . . . 5. *Spinis* vel *lorica* ſquamoſa munitus.	Echinus terreſtris Armadillo.
	Veſpertilio.	*Digiti* 5. . . . . 5. *Pes anticus* in alam expanſus. *Mammæ* 2. pectorales.	Veſpertilio. Felis volans *Seb.* Canis volans *Seb.* Glis volans *Seb.*
GLIRES *Dentes primores* 2. utrinque. *Pedes* multifidi.	Hyſtrix.	*Aures* humanæ. *Corpus* ſpinoſum.	Hyſtrix.
	Sciurus.	*Digiti* 4. . . . . 5. *Cauda* longiſſima lanigera.	Sciurus. . . . volans.
	Caſtor.	*Digiti* 5. . . . . 5. palmipes poſtice. *Cauda* horizontalis, plana, nuda.	Fiber.
	Mus.	*Digiti* 4. . . . . 5. *Cauda* teres, ſquamoſa, hirſuta.	Rattus Mus domeſticus. . . brachiurus. . . macrourus. Lemures. Marmota.
	Lepus.	*Digiti* 5. . . . . 4. *Cauda* breviſſima, villoſa.	Lepus. Cuniculus.
	Sorex.	*Digiti.* 5. . . . . 5. *Dentes* laniis adſunt.	Sorex.
JUMENTA. *Dentes primores* incerti, obtuſi. *canini* exerti, validi.	Equus.	*Mammæ* 2. inguinales. *Pedes* integri.	Equus. Aſinus. Onager. Zebra.
	Hippopotamus.	*Mammæ* 2. inguinales (*Ariſt.*) *Pedes* quadrifidi.	Equus marinus.
	Elephas.	*Mammæ* 2. pectorales. *Pedes* 5. callis inſtructi.	Elephas. Rhinoceros.
	Sus.	*Mammæ* 10. abdominales. *Pedes* biungulati: raro ſimplices.	Sus. Aper. Porcus. Babyrouſſa. Tajacu.
PECORA. *Dentes primores inferiores* tantum: *Superiores* nulli. *Pedes* ungulati.	Camelus.	*Cornua* nulla.	Dromedarius. Bactrianus. Glama. Pacos.
	Cervus.	*Cornua* annua, primum piloſa. ſolida, ab apice creſcentia. plurimis ramoſa: feminis rara.	Camelopardalis. Caprea. Axis. Cervus. Platyceros. Rheno. *Rangifer.* Alces.
	Capra.	*Cornua* ſurſum verſa. erecta, ſcabra.	Hircus. Ibex. Rupicapra. Strepſiceros. Gazella. Tragelaphus.
	Ovis.	*Cornua* retrorſum flexa intorta, rugoſa.	Ovis vulgaris. . . Arabica. . . Africana. . . Angolenſis.
	Bos.	*Cornua* antrorſum verſa, lunulata, lævia.	Bos. Urus. Biſon. Bubalus.
Ordines.	Genera.	Characteres Generum.	Species.

II. AVES.

Corpus plumoſum. *Alæ* duæ. *Pedes* duo. *Roſtrum* oſſeum. *Feminæ* oviparæ.

Ordines	Genera	Characteres Generum	Species
ACCIPITRES. *Roſtrum* uncinatum.	Pſittacus.	*Digiti* pedis antici 2. poſtici 2.	Pſittacus.
	Strix.	*Digiti* pedis antici 3. poſticus 1. quorum extimus retrorſum flexilis.	Bubo. Otus. Noctua. Ulula.
	Falco.	*Digiti* pedis antici 3. poſticus 1.	Aquila. Vultur. Buteo. Falco. Cyanopus. Milvus. Lanius. Pygargus. Niſus. Tinnunculus.
PICÆ. *Roſtrum* ſuperne compreſſum, convexum.	Paradiſæa.	*Pennæ* 2. longiſſimæ, ſingulares, nec alis, nec uropygio inſitæ.	Manucodiata. Avis Paradiſiaca.
	Coracias.	*Pes* 4dact. *Rectrices* exteriores gradatim breviores.	Pica.
	Corvus.	*Pes* 4dact. *Rectrices* æquales.	Corvus. Cornix. Monedula. Lupus. Glandaria. Caryocatactes.
	Cuculus.	*Digiti* pedis antici 2. poſtici 2. *Roſtrum* læve.	Cuculus. Torquilla ſ. Junx.
	Picus.	*Digiti* pedis antici 2. *Roſtrum* angulatum.	Picus niger. . . . viridis. . . . varius.
	Certhia.	*Pes* 4dact. *Roſtr.* gracile incurvum.	Certhia.
	Sitta.	*Pes* 4dact. *Roſtr.* triangulare.	Picus cinereus.
	Upupa.	*Pes* 4dact. *Caput* plumis criſtatum.	Upupa.
	Iſpida.	*Pes* 4dact. cujus digitus extimus medio adnectitur tribus articulis.	Iſpida. Merops.
MACRORHYNCHÆ. *Roſtr.* longiſſ. acut.	Grus.	*Caput* criſtatum.	Grus.
	Ciconia.	*Ungues* plani, ſubrotundi.	Ciconia.
	Ardea.	*Unguis* medius inferne ſerratus.	Ardea.
ANSERES. *Os* dentato-ſerratum.	Platelea.	*Roſtr.* depreſſo-planum, *apice* ſubrot.	Platea.
	Pelecanus.	*Roſtr.* depreſſum, *apice* unguiculato, inferne burſa inſtructum.	Onocrotalus.
	Cygnus.	*Roſtr.* conico-convexum.	Olor. Elder. Anſer. Anſ. Bernicla.
	Anas.	*Roſtr.* conico-depreſſum.	Anas fera. Glaucium. Boſchas. *A. Domeſt.* Penelope. Querquedula.
	Mergus.	*Roſtr.* cylindriforme, *apice* adunco.	Mergus. Merganſer.
	Graculus.	*Roſtr.* conicum, *apice* adunco.	Carbo aquat. Graculus aquat.
	Colymbus.	*Roſtr.* ſubulatum. *Pedes* infra æquilib.	Colymbus. C. minor. Podiceps. Arctica.
	Larus.	*Roſtr.* ſubulatum. *Pedes* in æquilib.	Cataracta. Larus. Sterna. Piſcator.
SCOLOPACES. *Roſtrum* cylindraceo-tereriuſculum.	Hæmatopus.	*Pes* 3dact. *Roſtri* apex compreſſus.	Pica marina.
	Charadrius.	*Pes* 3dact. *Roſtri* apex teres.	Pluvialis. Hiaticula.
	Vanellus.	*Pes* 4dact. *Roſtrum* digitis brevius. *Caput* pennato criſtatum.	Capella.
	Tringa.	*Pes* 4dact. *Roſtrum* digitis brevius. *Caput* ſimplex.	Tringa. Ocrophus. Pugnax. Glottis.
	Numenius.	*Pes* 4dact. *Roſtrum* digitis longius.	Gallinago. Limoſa. Arquata. Recurviroſtra.
	Fulica.	*Pes* 4dact. *Digiti* membranis aucti. *Caput* carnoſo-criſtatum.	Gallinula aquatica.
GALLINÆ. *Roſtrum* conico-incurvum.	Struthio.	*Pes* 2dact. abſque poſtico.	Struthio-camelus.
	Caſuarius.	*Pes* 3dact. abſque poſtico. *Caput* galea & palearibus ornatum.	Emeu.
	Otis.	*Pes* 3dact. abſque poſtico. *Caput* ſimplex.	Tarda.
	Pavo.	*Pes* 4dact. *Caput* corolla pennac. orn.	Pavo.
	Meleagris.	*Pes* 4dact. *Frons* papilla. *Gula* membrana unica longitudinali inſtructa.	Gallopavo.
	Gallina.	*Pes* 4dact. *Frons* membrana ſerrata. *Gula* membr. duplici longitud. inſt.	Gallina.
	Tetrao.	*Pes* 4dact. *Supercilia* papilloſa nuda.	Phaſianus. Urogallus. Tetrao. Bonaſia. Lagopus. Perdix. Coturnix.
PASSERES. *Roſtrum* conico-attenuatum.	Columba.	*Roſtr.* rectum, ad baſin furfuraceum. *Nares* oblongæ, membranula ſuperne inſtructæ.	Columba. Turtur. Palumbus. Oenas.
	Turdus.	*Roſtr.* parum convexum. *Plumæ* roſtri baſin tegunt.	Turdus. Merula.
	Sturnus.	*Roſtr.* rectum ſubteres. *Lingua* bifida cornea.	Sturnus.
	Alauda.	*Unguis* digiti poſtici digitis ipſis longior.	Alauda.
	Motacilla.	*Roſtr.* gracile. *Fauces* nigricant. *Lingua* apex bifidus laceratus.	Motacilla. Oenanthe. Merula aquatica.
	Luſcinia.	*Roſtr.* gracile rectum. *Lingua* apex bifidus laceratus.	Luſcinia. Ficedula. Erithacus. Troglodytes. Curruca *Rail.*
	Parus.	*Roſtr.* gracile. *Lingua* apex truncatus, 4 ſetis inſtructus.	Parus. P. caudatus. . . criſtatus.
	Hirundo.	*Roſtr.* gracile, ad baſin depreſſum, minimum: *rictu* ampliſſimo.	Hirundo. Caprimulgus.
	Loxia.	*Roſtr.* craſſum, magnum, breve, curvum, undique convexum.	Coccothrauſtes. Loxia. Pyrrhula.
	Ampelis.	*Roſtr.* craſſum, rectum. *Remigum* apices nonnulli membranacei.	Garrulus Bohem.
	Fringilla.	*Roſtr.* craſſum. *Maxilla* utraque alteram ſinu quodam ad baſin recipit.	Fringilla. Carduelis. Emberiza. Spinus. Paſſer.

III. AMPHIBIA.

Corpus nudum, vel ſquamoſum. *Dentes molares* nulli: *reliqui* ſemper. *Pinnæ* nullæ.

Ordines	Genera	Characteres Generum	Species
SERPENTIA.	Teſtudo.	*Corpus* quadrupedium, caudatum, teſta tectum.	Teſtudo teſſulata. . . . terreſtris. . . . marina. Lutaria.
	Rana.	*Corpus* quadrupedium, cauda deſtitutum, ſquamis carens.	Bufo. Rana arborea. . . aquatica. . . Carolina.
	Lacerta.	*Corpus* quadrupedium, caudatum, ſquamoſum.	Crocodilus. Alligator. Cordylus. Draco volans. Scincus. Salamandra aq. . . terreſtris. Chamæleo. Seps. Senembi *Mrg.*
	Anguis.	*Corpus* apodum, teres, ſquamoſum.	Vipera. Cæcilia. Aſpis. Caudiſona. Cobras de Cabelo. Anguis Æſculapii. Cenchris. Natrix. Hydrus.

AMPHIBIORUM Claſſem ulterius continuare noluit benignitas Creatoris; Ea enim ſi tot Generibus, quot reliquæ Animalium Claſſes comprehendunt, gauderet; vel ſi vera eſſent quæ de Draconibus, Baſiliſcis, ac ejuſmodi monſtris αἱ τερατολόγοι fabulantur, certè humanum genus terram inhabitare vix poſſet.

PARADOXA.

HYDRA corpore anguino, pedibus duobus, collis ſeptem, & totidem capitibus, alarum expers, aſſervatur Hamburgi, ſimilitudinem referens Hydræ Apocalypticæ à S. JOANNE CAP. XII. & XIII. deſcriptæ. Eaque tanquam veri animalis ſpeciem plurimis præbuit, ſed falſo. Natura ſibi ſemper ſimilis plura capita in uno corpore nunquam produxit naturaliter. Fraudem & artificium, cum Ipſi vidimus, dentes Ferino-muſtelini, ab Amphibiorum dentibus diverſi, facillime detexerunt.

RANA-PISCIS ſ. RANÆ IN PISCEM METAMORPHOSIS valdè paradoxa eſt, quum Natura mutationem Generis unius in aliam diverſæ Claſſis non admittat. Ranæ, ut Amphibia omnia, pulmonibus gaudent & oſſibus ſpinoſis. Piſces ſpinoſi, loco pulmonum, branchiis inſtruuntur. Ergo legi Naturæ contraria foret hæc mutatio. Si enim piſcis hic inſtructus eſt branchiis, erit diverſus à Rana & Amphibiis. Si verò pulmones, erit Lacerta: nam toto cælo à Chondropterygiis & Plagiuris differt.

MONOCEROS *Veterum*, corpore equino, pedibus ferinis; cornu recto, longo, ſpiraliter intorto, Pictorum figmentum eſt. MONODON *Artedi* ejuſmodi cornu gerit, cæteris vero partibus multum differt.

PELECANUS roſtro vulnus infligens femori ſuo, ut emanante ſanguine ſitim pullorum levet, fabuloſè ab iiſdem traditur. Anſam fabulæ dedit ſaccus ſub gula pendulus.

SATYRUS caudatus, hirſutus, barbatus, humanum referens corpus, geſticulationibus valde deditus, ſalaciſſimus, Simiæ ſpecies eſt, ſi unquam aliquis viſus fuit. *Homines* quoque *Caudati*, de quibus recentiores peregrinatores multa narrant, ejuſdem generis ſunt.

BOROMETZ ſ. AGNUS SCYTHICUS plantis accenſetur, & agno adſimilatur; cui caulis alterius plantæ è terra erumpens umbilicum intrat; idemque ſanguine præditus à feris devorari temerè dicitur. Eſt autem artificioſe ex radicibus Filicinis Americanis compoſitus. Naturaliter autem eſt *Embryo Ovis* allegoricè deſcriptus, qui omnia data habet attributa.

PHOENIX, Avis ſpecies, cujus unicum in mundo individuum, & quæ decrepita ex ferali buſto, quod ſibi ex aromatibus ſtruxerat, repueraſcere fabuloſè fertur, felicem ſubitura prioris vitæ periodum. Eſt verò PALMA DACTYLIFERA vid. *Kæmpf.*

BERNICLA ſ. ANSER SCOTICUS & CONCHA ANATIFERA è lignis putridis in mare abjectis naſci à Veteribus creditur. Sed fucum impoſuit *Lepas* interaneis ſuis penniformibus, & modo adhærendi, quaſi verus ille anſer *Bernicla* inde oriretur.

DRACO corpore anguino, duobus pedibus, duabus alis, Veſpertilionis inſtar, eſt *Lacerta alata*, vel *Raja* per artem monſtroſe ficta, & ſiccata.

AUTOMA MORTIS Horologii minimi ſonitum edens in parietibus, eſt *Pediculus pulſatorius* dictus, qui ligna perforat, eaque inhabitat.

REGNUM ANIMALE.

IV. PISCES.
Corpus apodum, pinnis veris instructum, nudum, vel squamosum.

V. INSECTA.
Corpus crusta ossea cutis loco tectum. Caput antennis instructum.

VI. VERMES.
Corporis Musculi ab una parte basi cuidam solidæ affixi.

PLAGIURI *Cauda horizontalis.*	Trichechus	Dentes in utroque maxilla. Dorsum impenne.	Manatus f. Vacca mar.	**COLEOPTERA.** *Alæ obtectæ duabus testis.*	Blatta	**5. FACIE ANTERIORI PAULO DECLIVI.** Elytra concreta, alæ nullæ. Antennæ truncatæ.	Scarab. tardipes. Blatta fœtida.	Gordius	Corpus filiforme, teres, simplex.	Seta aquatica. Vena Medina.
	Catodon	Dentes in inferiore maxilla. Dorsum impenne.	Cete Chlo.		Dytiscus	Pedes postici remorum forma & usu. Ant. setaceæ. Scuta apex biflorum.	Hydrocantharus. Scarab. aquaticus.	Tænia	Corpus filiculum, planum, articulatum.	Lumbricus longus.
	Monodon	Dens in superiore max. 1. Corpus impenne.	Monoceros. Unicornu.		Meloë	Elytra mollia, flexilia, corpore brevioris. Ant. moniliformes. Ex articulis oleum fundens.	Scarab. unctu. Scarab. medicus.	Lumbricus	Corpus teres, annulo prominentiâ cinctum.	Intestinum terra. Lumbricus latus. Ascaris.
	Balæna	Dentes in sup. max. corneis. Corpore supra impenne.	B. Grœnland. B. Finfisch. B. Musli. inf. Iubart. Ac.		Forficula	Elytra brevissima, rigida. Cauda bifurca.	Staphylinus. Auricularia.	Hirudo	Corpus inferne planum, superne convex.	Sanguisuga.
	Delphinus	Dentes in utraque maxilla. Corpore pinniformi.	Orca. Delphinus. Phocæna.		Notopeda	Pedibus in dorso cassi. Ant. explicantia.	Scarab. elastica.	Limax	Corpus inferne planum, superne conv. nuditate subinflatum.	Limax.
CHONDROPTERYGII *Pinnæ cartilagineæ.*	Raja	*Foramina branch:* subtus 5. Corpus depressum.	Raja clav. asp. læv. Acr. Squatino-Raja. Alcavela. Pastinaca mar. Rubecula. Torpedo. Bos Fœt.		Mordella	Cauda aculeo rigido simplici armata. Ant. filiform. brevis.	Negatur ab Aldrovando.	Cochlea	Testa univalvis, spiralis, uniloculuris.	Helix. Labyrinthus. Voluta. Cochlea varia.
	Squalus	*Foram. branch.* utrinq. 5. Corpus oblongum.	Lamia. Canicula. Zygæna. Centrina.		Curculio	Rostro productum, teres, simplex. Ant. clavatæ in medio Rostri positæ.	Curculio.			Buccinum. Lyra. Turbo.
	Acipenser	*Foram. branch.* utrinq. 5. Os edentul. tubulatum.	Sturio. Huso.		Baceros	Cornu 1. simplex, rigidum, fixum. Ant. capitatæ, exsertæ.	Rhinoceros. Scarab. monoceros.			Cassida. Strombus.
	Petromyzon	*Foram. branch.* utrinq. 7. Corpus bipenne.	Lampetra. Mustela.		Lucanus	Cornua 2. ramosa, rigida, mobilia. Ant. capitata, solacea.	Cervus Volans.			Fusus. Tessellatus. Murex.
	Lophius	*Caput trunciforme corporis depressi. Appendices barbiformes sub tuto plano positum.*	Rana piscatrix. Guacucuja.		Scarabæus	**1. ANTENNA TRUNCATA.** Ant. clavatæ solaceæ. Melolontha. Cornua nulla.	Scarab. pilularis. Melolontha. Dermestes.	Nautilus	Testa univalvis, spiralis, multilocularis.	Nautilus. Orthoceros. Lituus.
BRANCHIOSTEGI *Pinnæ ossibus, cartilag. branch. offic. & maxillæ.*	Cyclopterus	*Pinnæ ventrales in unicam circulariter conicretæ.*	Lumpus. Lepus mar.		Dermestes	Ant. clavatæ haerentibus perfoliatæ. Clypeus planiculum, emarginatus.	Cantharis fuliginos.			
	Ostracion	*Pinnæ ventrales nullæ.* Costa dura, & saepe aculeata.	Orbis div. sp. Pœr. triangul. Atinga. Nychio. Ostracion. Lagocephalus.		Cassida	Ant. clavatæ fabulatum. Clypeus planus, antice rotundatus.	Scarab. Clypeatus.			
	Balistes	*Dentes conspicui maxillæ. Scuta aequant robusti in dorso.*	Capriscus. Hollus. Capriscus. Caper.		Chrysomela	Ant. simplices, clypeo longiora. Corpus subrotundum.	Cantharellus.	Cypræa	Testa univalvis, convoluta, rima longitudinali.	Concha Veneris. Porcellana.
ACANTHOPTERYGII *Pinnæ ossibus, quarum spinosi aculeati.*	Gasterosteus	*Memb. branch. officosilis 3. Pinnæ laminis offeis inscr.*	Aculeatus. Pungitius.		Coccinella	Ant. simplices, breviflimus. Pedibus pullicis fultum.	Coccinella vulg.			
	Zeus	*Memb. branch. offic. 7. Squama lateliperis.*	Aper. Faber. Gallus mar.		Gyrinus	Ant. simpliers. Corpus breve, rotundo pollica fultum.	Pulex aquaticus. Pulex plutarum.	Haliotis	Testa univalvis, patula, leviter concava, perforata, ad unguem spiralis.	Auris marina.
	Cottus	*Membrana branch. offic. 6. Corpore aculeatim, corpore lævi.*	Cataphractus. Scorpio mar. Gobio fl. capit.		Necydalis	Ant. clavato-productae. Clypeus singulus, rotundatus.	Scarabæo-mordica.			
	Trigla	*Appendices ad pinn. rost. articulatae a vel 3.*	Lyra. Hirundo. Mulus barb. & rubusti.		Attalabus	Ant. simplices, cauthearha antennis ut-bicularibus, praeter abim. gloutilem.	Scarab. perlenfis.	Patella	Testa univalvis, concava, simplex.	Patella.
	Trachinus	*Operc. branch. aculeata. Oculi vicini in vertice.*	Draco. Uranoscopus.		Cantharis	**3. ANTENNA SETACEA.** Clypeus planus, imagine undique promin. Elytra flexilis.	Cantharis offic.			
	Perca	*Memb. branch. offic. 7. Pinnæ dorsales. 1 vel 2.*	Lucioperca. Cernua.		Carabus	Ante fine planus, marg. prostiuctre. Elytra flexilia.	Cantharellus noctidus. Conf carbo aurata.	Dentalium	Testa univalvis, teres, simplex.	Dentalium. Entalium. Tubus vermiculi.
	Sparus	*Opercula branch. squamosa. Labia dentes tegunt. Dentes molares obtusi.*	Salpa. Sparus. Mormyrus. Pagrus. Raja. Synagris. Dentex. Scarus. Papago. Papago.		Cicindela	Clypeus cylindraceus vel teres. Rostro vix prominente.	Cantharus Marinus.			
	Labrus	*Labia cerifa dentes teg. Cauda integra.*	Julis. Turdus diversae species.		Leptura	Clypeus fabricatus. Pedes longi. Corpus tenax.	Scarab. tenax.	Concha	Testa bivalvis.	Musculus. Vulva marina. Pinna.
	Mugil	*Memb. branch. offic. 6. Corpore toto squamosum.*	Cephalus.		Cerambyx	Clypeus ad latera tuberose prominet. Ant. corpore longitudine aequat, vel superant.	Capricornus.			Buccardium. Pecten. Chama.
	Scomber	*Memb. branch. offic. 7. Pinnæ dorsi 2. vel plures.*	Glaucus. Scomber. Trachurus Saurus. Amia. Thynnus.		Buprestis	Clypeus superne a punctis elevatis notatus.	Scarab. fulviescens.			Solenus. Tellina. Mya. Ostrea.
	Xiphias	*Rostrum apice emissforord. Pinnæ ventralis nullæ.*	Gladius.							Pecten. Mitella. Pinna.
	Gobius	*Pinna ventr. in 1 simpl. conica. Squama lipium.*	Gob. niger. Joco. Paganellus. Alb aa.		Papilio	*Rostrum spirale. Alæ 4.*	Papilio alis erectis. Psiche—volit. Phalæna—repens. Phalæna—compectis.			
MALACOPTERYGII *Pinnæ offeæ, quarum nullæ aculei.*	Gymnotus	*Absente branch. officuli 5. Foramen dorsalis nulla.*	Carapo.	**ANGIOPTERA.** *Alæ nectareo nuteo, clypeo obtecta.*	Libellula	*Cauda foliacea. Alæ 4. expansae.*	Puris. Virguncula.	Lepas	Testa multivalvis, valvulæ duabus plures.	Concha anatifera. Verruca testudin. Balanus marinus.
	Muræna	*Memb. branch. officuli. 10. Tubuli ab apice rostri 2.*	Anguilla. Conger. Muræna.		Ephemera	*Cauda fifola. Alæ 4. erectae.*	Musca Ephemera.			
	Blennus	*Pinnæ ventr. constant off. 2. Capite subrotundo declivis.*	Alauda non criff. & galer. Blennus. Gunnucrigera.		Hemerobius	*Cauda fifola. Alæ 4. compectie.*	Perla.			
	Gadus	*Memb. branch. offic. 7. Pinnæ dorsli. 2 vel 3.*	Asellus diversae species. Molucclus. Aeclatus rabus. Pollus. Limandis. Haploglossus. Bughali. fabra.		Panorpa	*Cauda chelat. Alæ 4. deflexa, refium.*	Mella Scorpionis.			
	Pleuronectes	*Memb. branch. offic. 6. Oculi ambo in eodem latere.*			Raphidia	*Cauda spinoli—linares. Alæ 4. Cap. com.*	Non fictus.			
	Ammodytes	*Pinna ventr. nulla.*	Ammodytes. Tobianus.		Apis	*Cauda aculeo simpli. Alæ 4.*	Castro. Vespa. Bombylius. Apis.	Tethya	Corpus forma variabile, molle, undum.	Tethya. Holothurion. Penna marina.
	Coryphæna	*Memb. branch. offic. 5. Pinna dorli a capite ad caudam.*	Hippurus. Pompilus. Novacula. Pastin.		Ichneumon	*Cauda aculeo punctio. Alæ 4.*	Musca div. spec. Muscca tripila.			
	Echeneis	*Stria transverfæ, asperæ, in fin supina capite porro.*	Remora.		Musca	*Stylus sub alis capitum. Alæ 2.*	Oestrum. Culex. Asilus. Tanutus. Tipula. Pumulactus.	Echinus	Corpus fabrotundum, testa tectum, aculeis armatum.	Echinus marinus.
	Esox	*Memb. branch. offic. 14.*	Lucius. Belone. Aeus marinus Spatanola.		Gryllus	*Pedes 6. Alæ 4. superiores cultiores.*	Gryllus domesticus. Gryllo—talpa. Locusta. Mantis.			
	Salmo	*Memb. branch. offic. 10-12. Corpus maculatum.*	Sturio. Trutta. Capito lacustr.	**HEMIPTERA.** *Alæ oblique deflexae, quadratim incumbenti convectæ.*	Lampyris	*Pedes 6. Clypeus planus. Alæ 4.*	Cicindela.	Asterias	Corpus radiatum, coxio tectum, scaturo.	Stella marina. Stella oligactis. St. pentadactylodes. St. polylactinoid.
	Osmerus	*Memb. branch. offic. 7—8. Dentes in max. lingu. palat.*	Epelanus. Saurus.		Formica	*Pedes 6. Alæ 4. cruciformes.*	Formica.			
	Coregonus	*Membr. branch. offic. 9. Appendices pinnaliformis.*	Lavaretus. Oxydendulum.		Cimex	*Pedes 6. Alæ 4. cruciformes. Styloms stylistome, restium.*	Cimex lectularius. Onopordon. Tipula aquatica. Brinchus.	Medusa	Corpus orbiculatum, gelatinosum, subtus filamentoluni.	Urtica marina. Urt. vermifcarnis. Urt. crinita. Urt. altrophya.
	Clupea	*Memb. branch. offic. 9. Venter ardlea ferratis.*	Harengus. Sprati. Encrasicolus Alosa.		Notonecta	*Pedes 6. quorum postici remorum figura & usu. Alæ 4. cruciatae.*	Notonecta aquatica.			
	Cyprinus	*Ossophthalmae Mogil. fine.* Brama. Capito. Corefinus. Thoc. Rutilus. Leucilius. Cobitis b.		Nepa	*Pedes 4. Frons chelifera. Alæ 4. crucif.*	Scorpio aquat.	Sepia	Corpus oblongum, interne offium, truncum octo artubus donatum.	Sepia. Loligo.
					Scorpio	*Pedes 8. Frons chelifera, aculeata. Alæ 4. letta.*	Scorpio terrestris.			
	Cobitis	*Caput compressum. Pinnæ dorsi & ventralis a dem a radiis distantis.*	Cobitis. Mustela.	**APTERA.** *Alæ nullæ.*	Pediculus	*Pedes 6. Antennæ capite breviores.*	Pediculus humanus. Ped. avium. Ped. pullimentos.	Microcosmus	Corpus variis heterogeneis tectum.	Microcosm marin.
	Syngnathus	*Opercula branch. ex lamina 1. Maxillis a lateribus clausae.*	Aous Aristot. Hyppocampus.		Pulex	*Pedes 6. filtatrices.*	Pulex vulgaris.			
					Monoculus	*Pes 1.? Antenna bifida.*	Pulex arboresf. fluxum. Monoculus Branch. Apus Frisch.			
					Acarus	*Pedes 8. articula 8 conflantes. Oculi 2. Ant. minima.*	Ricinus. Scorpio-araneus. Pedic. inguinalis. Pedic. Scrutuli. Pedic. scutatus. Acarus coccineum.			
					Araneus	*Pedes 8. Oculi commoniter 8.*	Araneus. Tarantula. Phalangium.			
					Cancer	*Pedes 12. priores thelliferentes.*	Cancer. Afleos. Pagurus. Squilla. Majas. Erratila. Guammarus.			
					Oniscus	*Pedes 14.*	Afelus offic. Afellus aquat.			
					Scolopendra	*Pedes 20. & ultra.*	Scolop. terrestris. Scolop. marina. Julus.			

REPTILIA. *Nuda, artubus distincta.*			
TESTACEA. *Habitatio Lapideis inferuata.*			
ZOOPHYTA. *Animalia plantis.*			

Plus, he tacked on a catch-all group of ten organisms, the Paradoxa, whose very existence he doubted.

Even though people in the early eighteenth century knew that humans were animals, they always studied them separately from the "beasts." Many were shocked when Linnaeus listed humans in the same kingdom as the beasts in his 1735 book.

◇◇◇

As for the mineral kingdom, Linnaeus divided it into three classes. The first contained rocks. The second included minerals and ores. The third was made up of fossils and sedimentary rocks called aggregates.

He taught his students that, although none of these was alive, they "grew"—not from eggs or seeds, as animals and plants did, but from different types of loose materials, such as sand or clay. He believed this "growth" could happen in one of two ways. Soils could combine with salts and transform chemically, or they could clump together and harden.

"It is beyond controversy," he wrote, that rocks "derive from soils, such as schists from vegetable boggy soil, whetstone from sand, marble from clay."

While Linnaeus believed rocks were simple elements and minerals were complex, today's geologists view them the other way around: minerals are the building blocks of rocks.

Linnaeus's classifications in this kingdom are no longer used, but he did get some things right. For instance, he correctly understood that corals were generated by animals and that their skeletal remains had once been part of living organisms. Also, he recognized an important point: that minerals are a necessary part of living things, but they themselves are not alive. Today we also know that when minerals in the soil undergo chemical weathering from rain and snow, they release many nutrients essential for plant growth. Plants absorb these nutrients, which then continue to move through the ecosystem as those plants are eaten by animals, and those animals are eaten by other animals higher in the food chain.

Linnaeus made several trips to Sweden's mining district, northwest of Uppsala. This was the place where his fiancée, Sara Lisa, had grown up and where her father was the community's sole doctor. Linnaeus visited smelting operations, a silver mine, and the Falun mine, which for years had been one of Europe's most productive copper mines.

While learning from Falun's mining experts, Linnaeus, whose chief interest still lay in botany and medicine, couldn't help but see the mine's effects on the local environment. The "poisonous, stinging, sulphurous smoke" rising from the mine in Great Copper Mountain was so corrosive that no plants grew in the area. He talked with miners and, to get a closer look at their working conditions, he descended into the 870-foot-deep mine.

As he climbed down the long twenty-step wooden ladders, fastened together end to end, they swayed and swung about. Below, twelve hundred miners crouched or crawled on hands and knees through low tunnels "filled with steam, dust and heat. . . . The drifts [passageways] are dark with soot," he wrote, "the floor of slippery stone, the passages narrow as if burrowed by moles, on all sides incrusted with vitriol, and the roof drips corrosive vitriolic water." The miners, despite wearing wool respirators over their mouths, suffered lung diseases from breathing stone dust, according to Linnaeus's diagnosis.

A few years later, in 1749, he studied coastal geology, as he journeyed through Sweden's southernmost province, Skåne, to survey its natural resources. North of Helsingborg, across the sound from Denmark, he counted the sedimentary strata exposed on a unique rock cliff by the sea. Linnaeus expressed amazement at the amount of time it would have taken for those layers to build up:

> I feel dizzy when I stand upon this hill and look down upon the long period of time which has passed like waves in the Sound, leaving behind only these faintest traces of the former world, and which can now only whisper when all else has become still.

The age of the earth was a hotly debated subject in the eighteenth century. Linnaeus and his European contemporaries were aware of Chinese estimates based on the recorded succession of their emperors that dated back 30,000 to 60,000 years, making the earth five to ten times older than the six thousand years estimated by biblical scholars. Cautious of questions that could put science and religion into conflict, Linnaeus wrote in an autobiography that he "would gladly have believed that the earth was older than the Chinese had claimed, had the Holy Scriptures suffered it." Using today's advanced technologies, scientists have dated those sedimentary strata exposed on the Helsingborg cliff back to the Jurassic Period, more than 150 million years ago.

◇◇◇

Despite his great interest in animals and minerals, Linnaeus's true passion since boyhood was the study of plants. For the plant kingdom he created a four-step system of classification.

First, he divided all plants into twenty-four broad classes. One class included plants without flowers; the rest, the flowering plants, he sorted into twenty-three classes according to the number and arrangement of their stamens.

Second, he divided each of the classes into smaller groups, called orders, by the number and arrangement of their pistils. It was convenient. Mathematical. Anybody could follow these first two steps simply by closely observing and counting the stamens and then the pistils.

Third, he divided each of the orders into the even smaller groups which Tournefort had called genera. Linnaeus kept most of the Frenchman's one-word genus names.

In the fourth and final step, he divided each genus into species, thus differentiating every specific type of plant from all the others.

For example, the pumpkin. If Linnaeus was looking at it for the first time, he would see that this type of squash was a flowering plant. When he went to count the stamens and pistils, he would see that they were located in different flowers on the same vine. Therefore it belonged in the class Monoecia, meaning "one house," with male and female flowers growing on the same

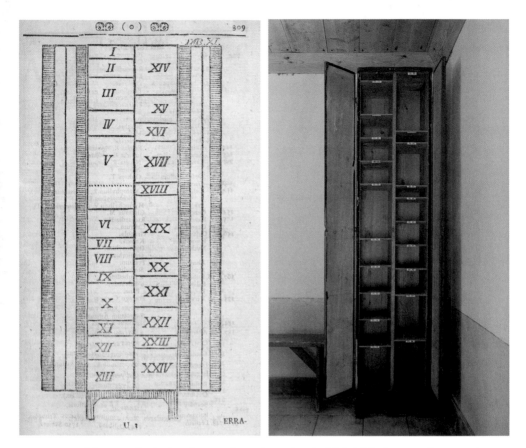

plant. When male and female flowers grew on separate plants, they belonged to a class he called Dioecia, or "two houses."

Linnaeus placed the dried pumpkin plant specimen on shelf XXI of his tall gray cabinet, with cucumbers, squash, melons, and all the other monoecious plants which had male and female flowers on the same plant.

The tulip has six stamens, so he placed it in the class Hexandria. The banana flower also has six stamens and joined the tulip on shelf VI. The holly, however, grows male and female flowers on completely separate plants, putting it in the class with the other dioecious plants. Linnaeus placed it on shelf XXII.

He called this plant classification system his "autopsy" of nature.

To make ideas memorable for his readers, Linnaeus used colorful metaphors. For instance, he imagined the plant kingdom as the temple of the goddess Flora, her head crowned with flowers. And when, during his travels in Sápmi, he spotted a pink-flowered plant growing on a rock in a marsh, and beneath it a newt, he named the plant *Andromeda*, after the mythical princess chained to a rock in the ocean guarded by a sea monster.

His fanciful analogies amused some people, but others were offended by the sexual references when he took the analogy to extremes. He compared plant reproduction with marriage—stamens as husbands and pistils as wives, petals as the bridal chamber. For instance, the class Monandria was "one husband in a marriage," Diandria was "two husbands in the same marriage," and when he reached Polyandria, an arrangement typical in poppy plants and linden trees, the analogy became "twenty males or more in the same bed with the female."

He explained his flowery analogy, writing that "The flowers' leaves . . . serve as bridal beds which the Creator has so gloriously arranged, adorned with such noble bed curtains, and perfumed with so many soft scents that the bridegroom with his

HOW LINNAEUS ORGANIZED PLANTS INTO CLASSES

To show the basics of this method, this chart lists examples of plants in each class by their current scientific and common names. Linnaeus's numerals correspond with Ehret's letters on the poster on page 124.

NUMBER OR ARRANGEMENT OF STAMENS	CLASS	SPECIES EXAMPLES
1	I. Monandria	*Hippuris vulgaris* (common mare's tail)
2	II. Diandria	*Syringa vulgaris* (common lilac)
3	III. Triandria	*Avena sativa* (common oat); *Iris versicolor* (blue flag)
4	IV. Tetrandria	*Cornus florida* (flowering dogwood)
5	V. Pentandria	*Myosotis palustris* (true forget-me-knot); *Limonium angustatum* (Carolina sea-lavender)
6: either equal, or if unequal having 3 long and 3 short stamens	VI. Hexandria	*Trillium grandiflorum* (white trillium); *Yucca glauca* (yucca or soapweed)
7	VII. Heptandria	*Aesculus glabra* (Ohio buckeye)
8	VIII. Octandria	*Vaccinium angustifolium* (lowbush blueberry); *Tropaeolum majus* (garden nasturtium or Indian cress)
9	IX. Enneandria	*Rheum rhabarbarum* (garden rhubarb)
10 or 11	X. Decandria	*Kalmia latifolia* (mountain laurel); *Sedum spathulifolium* (broadleaf stonecrop)
12–19	XI. Dodecandria	*Sempervivum globiferum* (hens and chicks; hen-widdies)
20 or more, filaments attached to calyx	XII. Icosandria	*Carnegiea gigantea* (saguaro cactus); *Rosa arkansana* (wild prairie rose)
20 or more, filaments not attached to calyx	XIII. Polyandria	*Magnolia grandiflora* (southern magnolia); *Eschscholzia californica* (California poppy); *Aquilegia coerulea* (Colorado columbine)

NUMBER OR ARRANGEMENT OF STAMENS	CLASS	SPECIES EXAMPLES
Stamens of markedly unequal length:		
2 long and 2 short	XIV. Didynamia	*Mentha arvensis* (wild mint); *Linaria vulgaris* (butter-and-eggs)
4 long and 2 short	XV. Tetradynamia	*Nasturtium officinale* (watercress)
Stamens united in the filaments or anthers:		
Stamens in one group or bundle	XVI. Monadelphia	*Camellia japonica* (camellia); *Thespesia grandiflora* (amapola); *Hibiscus brackenridgei* (pua aloalo)
Stamens in 2 groups	XVII. Diadelphia	*Trifolium pratense* (red clover); *Lupinus texensis* (bluebonnet)
Stamens in 3 or more groups	XVIII. Polyadelphia	*Citrus sinenis* (sweet orange)
Union of stamens confined to anthers	XIX. Syngenesia	*Helianthus annuus* (common sunflower); *Viola sororia* (common blue violet); *Taraxacum officinale* (common dandelion)
Stamens united with the pistil	XX. Gynandria	*Passiflora incarnata* (passionflower); *Cypripedium acaule* (pink lady slipper)
Stamens and pistils in different flowers:		
Male and female flowers on the same plant	XXI. Monoecia	*Cucurbita pepo* (pumpkin); *Quercus alba* (white oak)
Male and female flowers on different plants	XXII. Dioecia	*Populus deltoides* (Eastern cottonwood); *Ilex opaca* (American holly)
Male and female flowers mixed with hermaphrodite flowers	XXIII. Polygamia	*Musa acuminata* (banana); *Acer saccharum* (sugar maple)
No stamens:		
These plants have no proper flowers and reproduce with spores	XXIV. Cryptogamia (ferns, mosses, algae, lichens, fungi, mushrooms)	*Osmundastrum cinnamomeum* (cinnamon fern)

bride might celebrate their nuptials with so much the greater solemnity. When now the bed is so prepared, it is time for the bridegroom to embrace his beloved bride and offer her his gifts."

The names of most of his plant classes ended in "-andria," from the Greek word for "man"—Monandria, Diandria, Triandria. In this system, based on counting parts of the plant, the prefix was the total count: "mono-" (one), "di-" (two), "tri-" (three), and so on. The names of his plant orders ended in "-gynia," from the Greek for "woman"—Monogynia, Digynia, Trigynia. Cryptogamia—ferns, mosses, algae, and fungi—were "plants that marry secretly."

His so-called sexual system of plants turned a once-friendly correspondent, Johann Siegesbeck, director of the botanic garden in St. Petersburg, Russia, into a fierce and bitter critic. Calling it "lewd," Siegesbeck lashed out, saying, "Who would have thought that bluebells and lilies and onions could be up to such immorality?"

Linnaeus was extremely sensitive to criticism. He felt deeply stung and sought advice. A mentor urged him to never respond to critics. Linnaeus said nothing, but still could not resist temptation. On a packet of seeds that he'd named *Sigesbeckia* [sic] *orientalis* to honor Siegesbeck long before their fight, he now scrawled a new label—"*Cuculus ingratus*," meaning "ungrateful cuckoo." The packet made its way to the St. Petersburg Botanic Garden mixed in with other packets in a box that one of Linnaeus's students intended to trade for Russian seeds—and into the hands of Johann Siegesbeck. However, the feud did not stop there. In 1752, Linnaeus would rank the officers in "Flora's army." General Linnaeus put himself at the top, followed by various botanists as major generals, colonels, and chief officers. At the bottom was Sergeant-Major Siegesbeck.

Generally, though, when Linnaeus's fellow scientists saw the ease and practicality of his plant system, they began to use it. One fan, Jan Frederik Gronovius, who'd helped to finance the first edition of *Systema Naturae*, wrote to a colleague about the charts saying, "everybody ought to have them hanging in his study, like maps." This idea became reality when Georg Ehret painted a handsome poster which made the system's elegant simplicity even easier to grasp. The artist sold copies of his poster for two Dutch guilders. Every botanist in Holland bought a copy.

When Linnaeus published Ehret's poster in his book *Genera Plantarum* (The genera of plants), he used it without permission and failed to give the artist credit or payment. This unfair practice was common at the time. Ehret later griped that "When he was a beginner, [Linnaeus] appropriated everything for himself which he heard of, to make himself famous." Despite this, Ehret, who had similar grievances with other employers, remained friends with Linnaeus throughout his life.

Linnaeus wanted everybody to be able to learn about botany whether they were wealthy and educated or penniless and untrained, as he was as a boy.

His first-year university students often came to him with no previous education in science and little access to illustrated botany books. He worked hard to make his writing clear, concise, and in the simplest Latin. He avoided expensive copper-engraved images to keep costs low, so that each student could afford his

Doct: LINNÆI M.D.
METHODUS plantarum SEXUALIS
in SYSTEMATE NATURÆ
descripta

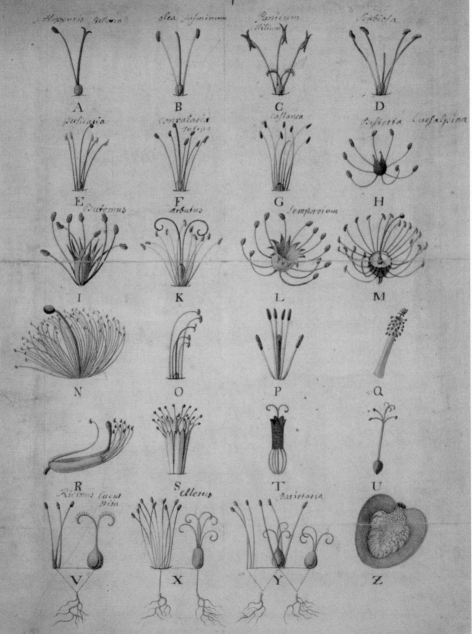

G.D. EHRET.
FECIT & EDIDIT
Lugd: bat: 1736.

own copy. One book, for instance, he insisted be priced at only two and a half shillings. Although this amount represented a few days' wages for most people, it was a small price compared with other books of the time.

Many of his books were short, easy to read, and compact—small enough to carry into the field. He published plant diagrams, as well as practical one-page instructions on how to plant a garden, set up a herbarium, pack seeds and live specimens for shipping, organize a field trip, and prepare for an expeditionary voyage.

His wildly popular plan for a "flower clock" reached an even wider audience of non-scientists. It was supposed to tell the time of day by the opening and closing of particular flower species, although different latitudes and seasonal variations made it impractical. Even so, many people had fun experimenting with it in their gardens.

Not all scientists were happy to have uneducated home gardeners and women dabbling in their profession. But Linnaeus was a science popularizer. He believed that even those not academically trained in science could be excited about nature.

◇◇◇

Meanwhile, Linnaeus continued building his worldwide network of prolific letter-writing scientists, a network he started with contacts from George Clifford's botanical exchange. Correspon-

OPPOSITE: Georg Dionysus Ehret's original hand-colored, engraved poster showing Linnaeus's system for classifying plants. Only this original drawing and two of the printed posters still exist.

dents from many countries, including botanists in charge of major European botanical gardens as well as amateur collectors, swapped plants with him and, in lengthy letters, debated ideas. In their letters back and forth, they greeted each other with extravagant compliments, following the custom of the day. However, as Linnaeus's student Johan Christian Fabricius observed, "He was generous with his praise because he himself loved to be flattered."

From the North American colonies, Alexander Garden, a medical doctor in South Carolina, corresponded with Linnaeus, as did John Bartram, a mostly self-educated botanist in Pennsylvania who ran a brisk global plant trade, even though he couldn't read Latin. Another correspondent, Cadwallader Colden, originally from Scotland, was a physician, surveyor, and New York's colonial lieutenant governor. He and his family lived on a 3,000-acre farm in the wilderness of the Hudson River highlands, sixty miles north of Manhattan. There, Colden translated Linnaeus's botanical Latin into English for his teenage daughter.

Like most women of her time, Jane Colden was never given the opportunity to attend school. But living in the wilderness, instructed and encouraged by her two well-educated parents, she became a skilled and careful observer. Once she mastered the Linnaean system, she quickly surpassed her father in botanical ability. John Bartram sent his son, William, to the Colden estate for a summer to learn about plants from her. Bartram and others praised her in letters to Linnaeus. She drew the plants and used the correct Linnaean names to describe dwarf ginseng, sarsaparilla, yellow lady's slipper, crinkleroot, blue

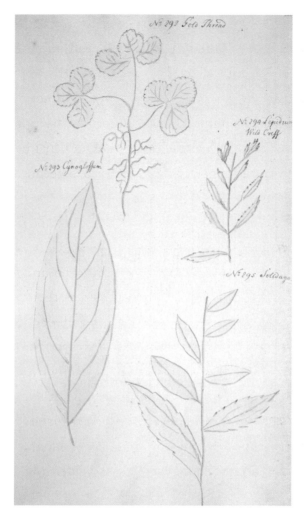

Drawings in Jane Colden's botanical journal,
including the plant goldthread.

lupine, goldthread, and some four hundred native plants on her
family's land.

Jane Colden was America's first female botanist. Linnaeus's
friend Peter Collinson, an amateur naturalist and London
merchant with business connections in North America, wrote

NATURAL VS. ARTIFICIAL

Linnaeus always knew that parts of his classification system were artificial: that is, not based on nature. His goal had always been a system based on natural relationships, but there were gaps in his knowledge that he knew created weaknesses in his system. Imperfect as it was, it stabilized science and gave the scientists who followed him time to collect more information and fix its weaknesses.

Within a few years of Linnaeus's death, scientists had replaced the more artificial parts of his system, responding to new facts. They added levels to his hierarchy, which now runs, from largest grouping to smallest: kingdom, phylum, class, order, family, genus, species, and subspecies.

Although Linnaeus's original, artificial system is no longer used, scientists still use his basic hierarchy and binomial nomenclature. His work enabled others to move forward with new and pioneering ideas that would eventually include evolution. Today, new technologies are helping scientists to better understand species and their genetic relationships. They are using new technologies to work toward a truly natural system—just as Linnaeus had hoped to create.

---

that she was "perhaps the only lady that makes profession of the Linnaean system." John Ellis, another British merchant, naturalist and a regular correspondent of Linnaeus's, believed that she had discovered a new species which she had called *Fibraurea* (goldthread). He and the others urged Linnaeus to name the plant after her. Coldenella, they suggested. "She deserves to be celebrated," Collinson wrote. It turned out that the plant had been discovered previously and had a name: *Helleborus*.

One of the very few women for whom Linnaeus named a plant genus was Lady Anne Monson. This English botanist, who lived in Calcutta, India, and had collected plants with Linnaeus's student Carl Peter Thunberg at the Cape of Good Hope, shipped specimens from her collections to Linnaeus. He named one of them *Monsonia*.

In all, Linnaeus exchanged more than four thousand letters, plus seeds and specimens, with six hundred correspondents.

By the 1740s, Linnaeus's organizing system was attracting people of all ranks and means in many countries. He was helping to make nature study popular across the world. However, as he and his students worked with his two-step process of organizing and naming, they ran into a snag. Long, convoluted Latin names were slowing down everyone's fieldwork. Step two—naming— proved to be Linnaeus's next dilemma. It was a problem he needed to fix.

7

LAST NAME, FIRST NAME

LAST NAME, FIRST NAME

The shorter the specific name, the better . . . it is foolish to do in more [words] what can be done by fewer.

—CARL LINNAEUS, PRINCIPLE NO. 291, *PHILOSOPHIA BOTANICA* (THE SCIENCE OF BOTANY), 1751

For thousands of years, people have given names to living things to identify individuals from the rest of a group. They are often two words. Shasta daisy. Woolly mammoth. German shepherd. Poison ivy. Silver birch. Norway spruce. Swedish ivy. Alpine gentian. Lapland rosebay. Lapland buttercup. Glacier buttercup.

These common names are almost always different among people who speak different languages. But even people who live just a few miles apart can have different names for the very same thing. One person's mountain lion is another person's cougar— and somebody else's puma.

Sometimes a common name hinted at what a plant looked like, where it came from, or how it was used.

But they were not good identifiers. Since plants provided food and most medicines used by humans, correct identification could be a matter of life or death. Some plants could make people healthy. Others could kill them. They needed to know which was which.

Often scientists in different places came across the same species. Each concocted a name for the plant. The result was that most plants wound up with a slew of scientific names in a variety of languages. The mishmash of names was confusing. For instance, one naturalist called the common wild briar rose *Rosa sylvestris inodora seu canina*, while another called it *Rosa sylvestris alba cum rubore, folio glabro.*

As explorers sailed home with boatloads of strange plants from foreign lands, the need for precise names to tell them apart became more urgent. So scientists coined names that were more informative, and that meant they grew even longer. By the eighteenth century, Aristotle's "asparagus," from the third century BC, had morphed into Linnaeus's long descriptive name, *Asparagus caule inermi fruticoso, foliis aciformibus perennantibus mucronatis termis aequalibus.* This was not just any asparagus; it was the one with a "spineless stem with shrubby, needle-like perennial leaves ending uniformly in short, sharp points."

Names served two purposes. They were full scientific descriptions—leaves, stems, roots, flowers, fruit, uses—and they were also labels—what you called the plants, how you referred to them.

What science needed was a consistent system of naming that could be understood by scientists all over the world.

However, researchers conducted fieldwork in the natural environment away from their workrooms and reference books. What researchers needed were names that were easy to remember and quick to write. This crisis of names was evident when Linnaeus lived in Holland, but the solution was not. Botany would have to wait, there being something more urgent brewing in Linnaeus's own life.

◇◇◇

In 1738, Dr. Boerhaave, wanting Linnaeus to settle in Holland, offered him the chance to join a Dutch expedition to the Cape of Good Hope and South America with the promise of a professorship afterward. Linnaeus turned him down. He was anxious to return to his fiancée. His three years were almost up, and he had heard that someone else was seeking to court Sara Lisa.

Linnaeus returned to Sweden, set up a medical practice in Stockholm, and began treating patients. On June 26, 1739, Carl Linnaeus and Sara Lisa Moraea said "I do" at her parents' home.

Two years later, in May 1741, Linnaeus succeeded his old professor, Olof Rudbeck the Younger, as professor of medicine at Uppsala. In October, he and Sara Lisa moved with their infant son, Carl, into the late professor's house. Dr. Rudbeck had left it as messy as "an owl's nest." They cleaned it up, modernized the house, and Linnaeus delivered his inaugural lecture on the importance of travel within one's own country.

In the midst of all the other work, Linnaeus began the big job of renovating and reorganizing the garden. This was the garden where he'd introduced himself to Professor Celsius, where he'd

Carl Linnaeus and Sara Lisa Moraea at the time of their wedding in June 1739.

led his first demonstration as a second-year student to an enthusiastic crowd, and where he would be inspired and employed for the rest of his life. He'd had enough of trekking in the Arctic and traveling abroad. He never set foot outside Sweden again.

◇◇◇

Carl Linnaeus's most lasting contribution to science would be his system for naming species. Like twentieth-century computer programmers who built search engines to find information on the internet using keywords, Linnaeus created a simple way to make a massive amount of information easily searchable—using keywords. At the time, he had no clue how revolutionary his idea was. For Linnaeus, it was no more exciting than a handy shortcut.

THE CHILDREN

Carl and Sara Lisa had five children who lived to adulthood: a son, Carl, and four daughters, Lisa Stina, Lovisa, Sara Stina, and Sophia. They lost two further children: Sara Lena, who died at two weeks, and Johannes, who died of fever at age three. When Sophia was born after a difficult labor, there were no signs of life. Linnaeus fought to save her, trying mouth-to-mouth resuscitation and then insufflation, a treatment in which medicinal smoke was blown into the nose. Finally, after fifteen minutes, the baby took her first breath. Sophia would always have a special place in his heart. As a toddler, she often walked across town with her father, his handkerchief tied around her head, to the university's lecture hall, where she would stand between her father's knees as he taught.

All the children heard their father's conversations with students, whether in the garden, at the supper table, or in the upstairs lecture room at home in Uppsala. But as was common then, boys were treated differently when it came to education. Linnaeus enrolled young Carl in the university at age nine. Girls did not usually attend school, and Linnaeus's daughters

Nobody knows exactly what inspired him. The idea might have sprung from confused reports sent in by the first generation of young globetrotting Linnaeans busily exploring the world's wild places under extreme conditions. Or the idea might have been due to a farm study conducted around Uppsala. Either way, even the complex name-phrases that Linnaeus himself had so carefully crafted were still as many as twelve Latin words long. Wherever his students were, the lengthy names made it hard for them to keep track of plants. Their field notes were a muddle.

were no different. Once when her husband was away, Sara Lisa enrolled Sophia in a school. When he returned, he took her out again. But he taught his daughters to read and write, and some botany.

One of the girls showed both special interest in her father's plants and a scientific aptitude. On a summer evening at Hammarby, right at dusk, Lisa Stina, then nineteen, noticed sparks of light, like tiny lightning flashes, emanating from nasturtium flowers in the garden. She made observations several nights in a row. Even though others who watched with her corroborated her story, Linnaeus, who'd been out of town, wasn't convinced until he saw the nasturtiums himself on two consecutive nights. He encouraged Lisa Stina to write up her results as a scientific paper, and it was published by the Royal Swedish Academy of Sciences. The famous German author Johann Wolfgang von Goethe, an admirer of Linnaeus, named the phenomenon after her. The effect was thought to be electricity passing through the flowers, but years later, the flashes were proved to be an optical illusion—caused by the way our eyes discern the flowers' colors at twilight—not bioluminescence.

◇◇◇◇◇◇◇◇◇◇◇◇◇◇◇◇◇◇◇◇◇◇◇◇◇◇◇◇◇◇◇◇◇◇◇◇◇◇◇

The farm study was conducted in 1748. Thirty exuberant students traipsed through tall grass after cows, goats, sheep, horses, and pigs. Their job—to identify plants eaten by the animals and those avoided—was not easy. Which plants did goats prefer to eat? Which did sheep steer clear of? Did the pigs, true to their reputation, eat everything in sight?

Questions about what animals chose to eat had intrigued Linnaeus since he made an expedition to the Swedish province of Dalarna and the Norwegian woods along its border in 1734. There he noticed that the pack horses, tethered in lush pasture, devoured most plants but avoided valerian, lily of the valley, loosestrife, and others that would be toxic to them. The horses seemed to easily recognize healthy food from noxious.

On the other hand, every spring in Sápmi, where the harsh climate made forage plants scarce, whole herds of cattle suffered excruciating deaths. No one could explain the mysterious losses. Nervous farmers blamed toxic water, spiders, or a return of the plague. After days of searching their pastures, Linnaeus had diagnosed the cause of death as poisonous water hemlock. The cows, ravenously hungry for fresh green food after months of dry winter feed, grazed outside. He inferred that they were unable to detect the hemlock's telltale turnipy smell underwater in the wet springtime soil.

Linnaeus guessed that farm animals, when not overly hungry, would choose wholesome plants over toxic ones, as the expedition horses had done in Norway. By pinpointing plants preferred or avoided, his team could advise farmers which plants would raise the healthiest, most useful livestock for farm work and market.

Sweden was a nation of farmers. What livestock ate mattered to everyone. Since it was then commonly assumed that plants, animals, and minerals were resources put on earth by God for the benefit of humans, Linnaeus believed a central purpose of natural science was to aid the economy. "An economist without knowledge of nature," he claimed, "is like a physicist without knowledge of mathematics." Sweden's faltering economy, the result of years of costly wars with its neighbors, was always in the back of his mind.

The study was straightforward. Each student was assigned one type of animal. Nineteen-year-old Pehr Löfling focused on goats. To record plant names, he and his classmates each carried an inkpot, pen, and paper, and possibly their professor's new 420-page field guide to native Swedish plants. This book included eleven hundred plants and gave each a full scientific description.

With the livestock roaming from place to place as they ate, Löfling and his fellow students had to look up and write down phrase-names, literally on the run. They knew many one-word genus names like *Achillea*, *Rudbeckia*, and *Salvia*, but it was impossible to memorize all the lengthy strings of Latin words that came after.

For instance, when a goat ate a dandelion, Löfling hastily copied down the name:

627. LEONTODON calyce inferne reflexo

This genus name, *Leontodon*, or "toothed lion," referred to the dandelion leaf's jagged shape. The rest meant that the flower's calyx, or leafy covering, was bent backward in the lower part. This time Löfling got off easy. At only four words, it was one of the shortest.

The students' frustrations no doubt reminded Linnaeus of his own childhood struggles trying to learn complicated Latin plant names. One summer, as a four-year-old, he hiked with his father, Nils, through the woods and fields to a neighborhood picnic on the other side of the lake. Every few steps he begged for the

Claſſis XIX.

SYNGENESIA
POLYGAMIA ÆQUALIS.

LEONTODON.

627. LEONTODON calyce inferne reflexo. *Fl. lapp.*
280. *Hort. cliff.* 386.

Lens leonis, qui Taraxacon officinarum. *Vaill. act.*
1721. *p.* 230.

Dens leonis latiore folio. *Bauh. pin.* 126.*Tournef.inſt.*468.

Dens leonis vulgi ſive Urinaria. *Lob. ic.* 432.

Dens leonis. *Till. ic.* 40.

Hedypnois. *Fuchſ. hiſt.* 680.

Exteris Piſſ en lit. *Weſtrogothis* Kopiſſ. *Oſtrobothnien-
ſibus* Smörblomſter.

Habitat *in paſcuis ubique.*

Pharmac. TARAXACI *Radix*, *Herba*, *Aqua.*

628. LEONTODON calyce toto erecto hiſpido, foliis hiſpidis dentatis integerrimis. *Hort. cliff.* 386.
Act. ſtockh. 1741. *p.* 203. *Roy. lugdb.* 122.

Taraxaconoides perennis & vulgaris. *Vall. act.* 1721.
p. 232.

Dens leonis, foliis hirſutis & aſperis. *Tournef. inſt.* 468.

Hieracium aſperum, folio magno dentis leonis. *Bauh.
pin.* 127.

Hieracium, caule aphyllo, hirſutum. *Bauh. hiſt.* 2.
p. 1037.

Habitat *Wadſtenæ in* Oſtrogothia.

629. LEONTODON calycibus erectis, foliis glabris
dentatis integerrimis, pedunculis ſqvamoſis.

Crepis foliis longis dentatis linearibus, caule decli-
nato ſubnudo. *Hort. cliff.* 386.

Scorzoneroides chondrillæ vel coronopi folio pene
aphyllocaulos. *Vaill. act.* 1721. *p.* 273.   Scor-

A page from Linnaeus's field guide to Swedish plants. Entry 627 was one species of dandelion. After each descriptive name, he inserted descriptions by Vaillant, Tournefort, and other botanists. Then he listed common names. For instance, the French name *piss en lit*, meaning "wet the bed," came from the practice of giving dandelion tea, a diuretic, to children early in the day to prevent bedwetting at night. Linnaeus also included the habitat of each plant and its pharmaceutical uses. Entry 628 was a different species of dandelion.

name of a plant. What's this? What's that? His father answered patiently . . . until the boy asked about the same plants over and over again. Nils warned that he would stop telling him the names if he did not start remembering them. The little boy put his mind to it, and before long he knew every one.

Linnaeus empathized with his students. He had been experimenting with a way to speed up their note-taking. He showed them his shortcut: just the genus name plus its number from the field guide.

So now, as young Löfling chased after a goat to figure out which of the three dandelion species it was eating, he scribbled:

Leontodon, **No. 627**

This was a little easier than before, but Löfling still had to look up the number while he was in the field. Later he would use the number to look up the full name for his final report.

In the meantime, the students scrambled to outdo one another. They kept track using a code:

1 – for a plant the animal ate;

0 – not eaten;

1 + 0 – sometimes eaten, sometimes refused;

1 0 – eaten fresh but not dried;

1 1 – eaten with great pleasure.

Pehr's goats especially enjoyed blue fieldmadder, with its little blue flowers, and queen of the meadow.

The team conducted 2,300 tests, some repeated as often as twenty times. Pehr Löfling, for instance, checked his results by mixing a test plant into a pile of known goat-favorites. Of all the animals, the goats were the least picky eaters. Which were the most selective eaters? Surprisingly, the pigs. They turned up their snouts at 171 kinds of plants and ate only 72.

When the students turned in their reports, Linnaeus prepared a chart. Using the same codes they had used, he tabulated the results in separate columns for cows, goats, sheep, horses, and pigs. To list the plants, in the first column he wrote a number. In the second column, next to the genus, he wrote one word, usually an adjective, for each of the species in that genus:

[#]   [Genus]   [species]   627. Leontodon taraxacum

He looked for a key adjective in each existing lengthy description in his field guide. He wanted a single distinctive word that pertained to one species of plant and was unique to that species only and easy to remember. It was supposed to be a temporary nickname.

After the study was complete, Linnaeus continued to experiment with names. Then he streamlined the shortcut: he dropped the number entirely. This left two words, the genus name followed by one word. Together, these two key words became the binomial (from Latin, bi- meaning "two," and -nomial meaning "name"). The first word described the whole group, or genus, and the second word limited the name to one member of that group, the species. The second word was often a physical or geographic characteristic. It was simpler to remember than a number. This

Linnaeus's notebook from the farm study. Columns show the eating preferences of cows (Boves), goats (Caprae), sheep (Oves), horses (Equi), and pigs (Sues).

made his students' fieldwork quicker and easier. It eliminated the need to lug around a field guide.

Binomials had been used before; Linnaeus didn't invent them. However, he was the first to apply them consistently. What he did was standardize the naming process and make it universal. Previously a scientific name had served as both a name and a full description. Linnaeus separated those two functions. Now the name was only a label. It had only one job. There was no need to scribble down details out in the field.

This change also separated the collecting of information from its analysis. Again Linnaeus was shaking up another long-standing way in which he and his fellow scientists worked.

He explained that adding the species name to the genus was like putting "a clapper into a bell." Without a clapper to strike the bell, a bell makes no sound and cannot do its job. The second word called out clearly one distinguishing feature of each particular species. *Acer rubrum*, red maple. *Theobroma cacao*, "food of the gods," cocoa. *Citrus sinensis*, sweet orange (*sinensis* means "Chinese"). Even the potato got a new scientific name. In his nomenclature, the official scientific name was *Solanum caule inermi herbaceo, foliis pinnatis integerrimis*. Its new nickname was simply *Solanum tuberosum*, "fleshy tuber."

◇◇◇

Five years later, in his book on the species of plants, *Species Plantarum* (1753), Linnaeus listed the full descriptive plant names in alphabetical order together with their simple two-word nicknames: the genus name plus what he called a trivial name for the species. He had often chosen them quickly. That he called it "trivial" shows how unimportant he thought this shortcut was. He still considered the longer version to be the one true and permanent name. Not everyone agreed with Linnaeus's ideas, but more scientists began using his system, and its popularity soared. For the first time in history, a scientific name would be consistent and universal no matter which country was home to the scientist who coined it.

Linnaeus set rules for creating both genus and species names. The format was always the same:

Genus + species = binomial name

The genus name was like a person's last name—for example, Lincoln—which is given to all the members of a particular family. The species name was like a person's first name, given at birth— Abraham, for example—which distinguishes that child from all the people related to him, in other words, from his parents and siblings who share the same last name. To Linnaeus, species were the basic units of life. The scientific name was presented "last name, first name." Lincoln, Abraham.

In addition, all Linnaeus's descriptions were written in the same scientific language, based on Latin and Latinized Greek root words. He spelled out scientific definitions and listed rules for creating standardized names, such as this one:

Names used by the ancients, that are 1-1/2 feet long, and which constitute descriptions instead of definitions, are to be abhorred.

He kept many established genus names but avoided those that "are difficult to pronounce." Some scientists had concocted names by lumping together several Latin and Greek descriptive words into a single word. These were very long. Linnaeus warned that words with more than twelve letters or several pairs of consonants were "liable to damage the throat of the speaker." He even gave examples: *Hypophyllocarpodendron*, *Coriotragematodendros*, *Acrochordodendros*, *Stachyarpogophora*, and *Orbitochortus*. He also ruled out "disgusting" names and gave examples. One plant, when crushed, gave off an awful odor. Somebody had named it *Galeobdolon*. The name meant "weasel-stink."

The names did not always describe physical properties. He often demoted old genus names, such as *Galeobdolon*, but preserved them as species names so apothecaries would still recognize plants they commonly used to treat illnesses. Since he had to come up with thousands of distinct names for plants and animals, his prolific reading sometimes fired up his imagination. He called butterflies after gods in Greek and Roman mythology and heroes of the Trojan War. He named plants after important botanists—living and dead—and his students. He frequently used names to celebrate people who had discovered the species.

Colleagues and his intrepid student-travelers shipped him boxes, crates, and packets of new species and seeds from distant places. They were dispatched from Indonesia, India, Egypt, Syria, Cyprus, Turkey, Yemen, and Iran; in Europe, Slovenia, Spain, Italy, Russia; and in the Americas, Suriname, Colombia, Venezuela, the West Indies, Pennsylvania, Virginia, Quebec. He rewarded some contributors by naming a plant or animal genus after them—such as the fragrant tropical shrub *Gardenia*, after naturalist and colonial physician Dr. Alexander Garden of Virginia. Then there were *Bartramia*, *Coldensonia* (after Jane Colden's father, not Jane), and *Collinsonia*.

His professor, Olof Rudbeck the Younger, was celebrated in the name of the black-eyed susan, *Rudbeckia*. Linnaeus named another genus *Celsia*, after his mentor Olof Celsius and his nephew Anders.

He named the mountain laurel *Kalmia* after his student Pehr Kalm, who explored North America. He named a tropical Spanish plant *Loeflingia* after Pehr Löfling, the enthusiastic young goatherder who later died while exploring Venezuela. And he named a beautiful umbellate plant *Artedia* after his dear friend Peter Artedi, who had been fascinated by the umbrella-like plants. Native to Cyprus, Israel, and the eastern Mediterranean, this annual—meaning it lasts only a year—was short-lived like Artedi. Also like its namesake, the genus *Artedia* contained only one species; it was one of a kind.

Sometimes names told memorable stories. A plant that could not tolerate too much water was named after Elias Tilliander, an Uppsala student who was so terrified by a stormy crossing of the Gulf of Bothnia that, on his return trip home, he traveled by land—an extra 1,800 miles—and changed his name to Tillandz, meaning "by land." *Tillandsia*, commonly called an airplant, grows attached to other plants and takes moisture and nutrients from the air.

During his lifetime, Linnaeus described and coined names for 7,700 plant and 4,400 animal species. He insisted this system be founded on direct, firsthand observation. So he studied each species using live or preserved specimens, drawings, and descriptions made by trusted global correspondents. He grew many rare plants in his own gardens. He peered through a microscope to name an amoeba *Chaos chaos*, Latin for "shapeless mass."

Linnaeus's landmark two-part name format was not an invention. It was actually a technological tool. What made it different from the two-word folk names already used by people around the world? Linnaeus's scientific names were precise, consistent, and in a single universal language. Since it was Latin, he expected all scientists would be able to understand it, no matter what language they spoke in their everyday lives. Plus, he used a common vocabulary with definitions that were standardized and consistent.

This naming system was a convenient way of organizing data so that information could be found more quickly. Binomial nomenclature—two-word naming—was an indexing tool that vastly simplified work. Linnaeus was making the most of his student support staff, and those hardworking students were grateful. Now they could finish more work in less time.

There was one plant that stumped him, though. What could he call a plant that was troublesome beyond words?

Monster.

Herbarium specimen sheet from the Natural History Museum, London.
Linnaeus named this umbellate plant *Artedia squamata* for his late friend
Peter Artedi.

INNOVATIONS
IN PAPER TECHNOLOGY

Linnaeus had to sort through and describe the constant rush of incoming plants, animals, and information. Despite taking quick power naps to refresh himself, the workload was stressful. He told a friend, "I feel like a tired horse who does not feel like obeying the whip." Over the years, he simplified his task by coming up with several paper technologies which changed the way botanists kept track of information and specimens. While they look obvious now, at the time they were revolutionary.

His first innovation was the use of loose herbarium sheets. For years, Linnaeus and his fellow botanists had glued dried plant specimens, two or three to a page, then bound them together as books. The problem was that newly found plants could not be added into books that were already bound, and the order in which the plants were arranged couldn't be changed. New specimens required new books.

Using isinglass, a paste made by boiling out a gooey substance from the swim bladders of freshwater sturgeon, Linnaeus began placing one specimen on a sheet. Only one. And he left the pages loose.

A second innovation was his cabinets. In order to organize all those loose sheets of paper, Linnaeus hired a local wood-worker to build three eight-foot-tall cupboards, 16 inches wide by 12 inches deep, with folding doors. Each cupboard could hold 6,000 loose sheets of paper, which meant 6,000 dried plant specimens. Linnaeus could relocate a plant to make room for the steady arrival of new discoveries at any place within the system.

Later in life, feeling overwhelmed by "information overload," Linnaeus came up with a more flexible way of looking at large masses of data. His third innovation was to cut paper into little slips 3 x 5 inches (7.5 x 13 cm). At the top of each slip, he wrote a genus name, then briefly described one species. He could file these, easily change their order, or spread them out on a table to analyze relationships. Today we call these slips of paper index cards.

In a time- and paper-saving innovation, Linnaeus began in 1751 to use the alchemical symbols that he had learned as a child in a new way—to indicate gender in plants. These symbols were letters from an ancient alphabet that medieval alchemists had adoped to abbreviate the names of metals.

♂ For male, Linnaeus used the symbol for iron, the hard metal that alchemists associated metaphorically with Mars, the god of war and agriculture.

♀ For female, he used the symbol for copper, the softer metal they associated with Venus, the goddess of love and fertility.

He was the first to use these symbols in the biological sciences.

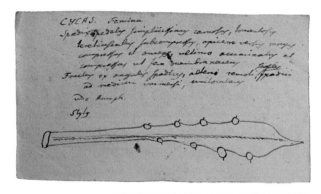

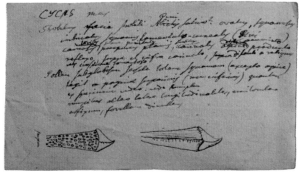

Examples of Linnaeus's "index cards," paper slips used to record and organize information as he prepared the twelfth edition of his book *Systema Naturae* in the 1760s.

〰〰〰〰〰〰〰〰〰〰〰〰〰〰〰〰〰〰〰〰〰〰〰〰〰〰〰

NAMES NOW

Linnaeus's book *Species Plantarum*, published in 1753, is considered to be the starting point for modern botanical naming. Any plant name used before the book's appearance became obsolete—even those coined by Linnaeus himself. In his tenth edition of *Systema Naturae*, published in 1758–59, he also established binomials for animals. That book became the starting point for modern zoological naming. By convention, the names are italicized. The genus name is capitalized and comes first; the species, uncapitalized, comes second. Even today, Linnaeus's system means that a scientist anywhere in the world, speaking any language, can use a two-word scientific name to find exactly the right plant or animal. The beauty of the system is its simplicity.

Three hundred years after Linnaeus's landmark innovation, botanists continue to change names and groupings as they learn more about genetic relationships through DNA testing, gene mapping, and other modern technological advances. But the majority of the thousands of plants described by Linnaeus are still recognized by the names he gave them.

History can be seen in the names themselves. Each one officially ends with the name or abbreviation of the person who coined it. Many are still followed by the simple, most famous initial of all: "L."

8

◇◇

THE MOST CONTROVERSIAL PLANT

Fantastic . . . unparalleled in botany . . . no less remarkable than if a cow gave birth to a calf with a wolf's head.

—CARL LINNAEUS, DISSERTATION, "PELORIA," 1744

"Here is something remarkable."

The note came tucked in a package from Linnaeus's colleague and old friend Olof Celsius. Inside, a pressed plant was glued onto an herbarium sheet.

Just an ordinary *linaria*, Linnaeus thought at first. Nothing special. It was native to many parts of Europe. Folks who spoke English called it toadflax, Jacob's ladder, or butter-and-eggs. In Sweden people knew it as *gulsporre*, meaning "yellow spur." It popped up everywhere along dusty cartways and in dry, rubbly fields. This was hardly a "remarkable" find.

But on closer examination, the flowers were all wrong. They looked as if they had been turned inside out.

It was the fall of 1742, and one of Celsius's students claimed he had found it while scouting specimens over summer vacation. He lived on South Gåsskäret, a speck of an island in the archipelago of 24,000 islands that dot the Baltic Sea off Stockholm's rocky coast.

In only his second year as a professor at Uppsala, Linnaeus was already considered the expert. Despite his commanding knowledge of flowers, this one stumped him. He was suspicious. Maybe it was a practical joke—flowers plucked from some other species and glued onto an ordinary *linaria* stem? Students often pulled pranks and Linnaeus was known to enjoy a good laugh. This would not be the first time somebody had tried to fool him. Maybe the plant had come from the Cape of Good Hope, Japan, or Peru. He found it hard to believe it had come from Sweden, whose plants he knew so well.

Normally a *linaria* flower had one cone-shaped spur. The spur was like a bottle into which a bumblebee would stick its strawlike proboscis for nectar. To reach the spur, the bumblebee first had to squeeze through the petals into the flower. Once inside, it pushed its way past stamens loaded with pollen, and the dusty yellow pollen brushed off onto its fuzzy back. When the bee entered the next flower, the pollen from the first flower rubbed off the bee's back onto the second flower's sticky pistil, pollinating it. Then and only then could the flower's seeds develop. That was how it was supposed to work.

However, when Linnaeus inspected one of these strange flowers, things were different. Instead of one spur, as in a normal *linaria* flower, there were five, like the arms of a starfish! Instead

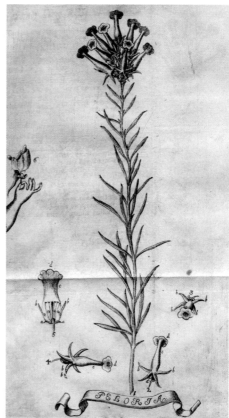

LEFT: A common *linaria* with normal flowers, each with one pointed spur. *RIGHT*: The mystery plant *peloria* with closed-up petals and five spurs on each flower, as pictured in Linnaeus's dissertation.

of halves that mirrored each other (like a chair), it had identical parts radiating around a center point (like a stool).

More importantly, the petals were not open for the bumblebee. They were sealed up, as tight as a Sami drum. There was no way for a bee to get inside to feed on nectar. Since the bumblebee could not pollinate the plant, Linnaeus assumed that the plant could not reproduce. So where did this plant come from? How could it even exist?

On the outside, he saw no evidence of a trickster's glue holding the flowers to the stem. When he dissected one of the flowers, what he found was equally strange. Inside was an internal structure he had never seen before in any other plant in that genus.

What Linnaeus had expected to find was two long and two short stamens. This would have meant it belonged with snapdragons, foxgloves, and other plants with four stamens in the genus *Antirrhinum*, the class Didynamia. But this flower had five stamens all the same length. He tried fitting it with other plants with five stamens, but it was nothing like the potatoes, primroses, heather, and others in that class either.

This was a head-scratcher. The bizarre plant broke all the rules he had laid out so carefully. His system was based on flower structures which he found repeated in plants from all over the world. Every flowering plant fit into these standard patterns . . . until this one. It did not fit anywhere. What could explain this mystery?

Linnaeus considered three options:

1. A species never seen before? Highly unlikely. Since Linnaeus and his fellow botanists knew almost every kind of plant growing in Sweden, he confidently ruled out that it was previously undiscovered.

2. A hybrid plant? Possibly. Scientists at the time recognized the existence of animal hybrids like the mule, the result of the union of a donkey and a horse. However, there was little discussion about whether the pollen of

one plant could fertilize a different kind of plant. There was no talk of whether such a union could produce a new plant species.

To be considered a species, a living thing had to be able to produce young like itself. Since the mule was sterile and could not produce little mules like itself, this animal hybrid was not a species. Therefore, the mule was no threat to the widely-held belief called the "fixity of species"—that all the plant and animal species in the world were created by God at once at the beginning of time. Most eighteenth-century Europeans held this basic view of the natural world. Linnaeus had learned it from his father. It was taught in every school he ever attended. He himself taught it to his own students.

3. A newly created species? Highly unlikely—unthinkable even.

Celsius's student confirmed that these strange plants were thriving in their island habitat. This meant to Linnaeus that the plants must be fertile, because they were producing similar young plants somehow. If this was a fertile hybrid, it would have to be a brand new species . . . one that had come into existence after Creation. Most people at the time considered this impossible. To say otherwise would have been dangerously close to heresy. Pursuing this radical idea would present big, messy complications for Linnaeus, both personally and professionally.

It was like running in the dark along the edge of a cliff. Linnaeus did not know where it would take him. It was unsettling.

Linnaeus wanted to see a live specimen. However, he did not visit the island site himself. Perhaps this was because traveling to the island would have taken a couple of days and this was the start of the school year, always a hectic time. Plus, the plant bloomed in late summer, and autumn was creeping toward winter. It is even possible he did not want evidence that would confirm his troubling suspicion that this could be a new species. No one knows why he didn't go.

Instead, he asked Celsius's student to return to the original habitat as soon as he could and, this time, dig up living plants with roots attached. He needed answers.

When the live specimens arrived, he immediately transplanted them in the university botanic garden. He watched and waited as their tender roots took hold. The plants survived just long enough to be studied.

During the next two years, Linnaeus agonized over what he thought he had seen and what it could mean. He wondered whether this was a fertile cross between a common *linaria* and some unknown plant. Even though his living specimens died off, he had seen fully developed seeds inside the flowers. And even though he did not try to grow those seeds, this observation convinced him that they were fertile, could have germinated, and could have grown into young plants similar to the parent plant.

However, his theory was complicated by two unresolved problems. First, he could not determine the other parent plant of the cross. Second, because he did not try to grow any seeds, he was operating on an untested hunch. If its seeds could grow into new, similar plants with five stamens and five spurs, he would be forced to conclude that a new species could originate in nature. Unlike a sterile animal hybrid, a fertile hybrid plant would be a new species.

If Linnaeus had traveled to the island and seen the abundant root structures himself, he would have realized that this plant did not always need seeds to reproduce. With a little digging, he would have traced the stems of these new plants back down into the soil to their source—horizontal rootlike structures coming from the *linaria* plants. He would have recognized that this growth was similar to ivy and pachysandra—and bananas. This type of underground stem, a rhizome, could send up shoots and send down new roots, invading an area by starting lots of new plants. No seed required.

Since Linnaeus did not travel to the island, he saw no other possible verdict: He was convinced that this was a newly-formed plant produced by the union of two different kinds of plants, and that it could produce young plants like itself. It was, he determined, a new species.

This was an extremely risky hypothesis. The theological implications were disturbing. It challenged the idea that no new species could emerge after the Creation. It derailed his own long-held belief that species could never change. Linnaeus named this new plant *peloria*, from the Greek word *pelor*, meaning "monster."

He wrote that a new species of plant growing from a common *linaria* would be "strange and unbelievable . . . it would not appear to be a greater miracle than if apple trees were to produce daffodils." He continued:

Nothing can, however, be more fantastic than that which has occurred, namely that a malformed offspring of a plant [differs from its mother plant and its entire class, making it] an example of something that is unparalleled in botany.

Yet, unless God had formed this species on that island off Stockholm's coast, Linnaeus admitted that an important mystery remained. "[What causes] the transformation of Linaria into Peloria is to us still unknown." He used the Latin word *mutatae*, or "mutates," by which he simply meant "changes."

◇◇◇

Linnaeus presented his ideas in a written dissertation. Following the standard protocol of the time, he dictated his ideas to one of his students. The student, Daniel Rudberg, then had to translate it from Swedish into proper Latin, publish it at his own expense, and defend his professor's conclusions before a faculty examining committee. The purpose was to test the student on his ability to successfully argue the position in Latin. On December 19, 1744, his student presented Linnaeus's controversial theory.

Linnaeus concluded in his dissertation:

If with certainty it could be established that Peloria is a hybrid herb that traces its origin from Linaria and another plant, then, a new truth from this would emerge within the plant kingdom . . . If [common] Linaria does not arise again from Peloria, a fantastic conclusion follows as a consequence, namely that it can occur that new species arise within the plant kingdom . . .

The theory—that a hybrid plant was capable of reproducing—intrigued some people and infuriated others.

"Your Peloria has upset everyone," warned Johan Browallius. Linnaeus's friend from Falun was now a natural history professor in Finland and later would become a Lutheran bishop. "[B]e wary of the dangerous sentence that this species had arisen after the Creation," he wrote. Do not, Browallius stated flat out, reach that conclusion. They were both well aware that only a hundred years earlier the Church of Rome had condemned Galileo's work in astronomy. History was filled with thinkers who had been persecuted for introducing new ideas.

Browallius urged Linnaeus to back off. He reasoned that all Linnaeus had done was organize plants into groups to make them easier for students to learn. Making groups is a human activity. Humans make mistakes.

However, Browallius advised, if Linnaeus insisted on rebelling against a commonly accepted natural law, he should follow the rule of the English physicist Isaac Newton. Newton maintained that the only way to disprove a natural law based on other people's experiences is to prove it wrong with one's own. In other words, he was suggesting that Linnaeus prove his theory by planting seeds and showing that they would grow.

This was good advice. Linnaeus didn't take it. There is no evidence that Linnaeus planted any seeds or conducted experiments to prove his *peloria* theory. He based his conclusions solely on his observations of the dried plant and the ones that were transplanted and grew for a short while in his garden in 1742.

That seems surprising to us today. In the mid-eighteenth

century, Linnaeus's English and French counterparts experimented and observed as part of their routine, following an empirical method. On the other hand, Swedish scientists still operated under a scholastic method, that is, they based their deductions on theoretical principles found in the writings of Aristotle and others, instead of observation and experimentation.

Although he did not try to grow the seeds, he did send to others the few seeds he had available. While rumors of a backlash rumbled, Johann Gmelin, a German botanist working in St. Petersburg, Russia, wrote Linnaeus a letter of support. Gmelin was convinced that new plants could come from a union of different species. In fact, he had evidence that the genus *Delphinium* also produced weird hybrids. Gmelin and others begged Linnaeus to send them *peloria* seeds and dried specimens.

◇◇◇

Linnaeus predicted that one of the great scientific efforts of the future would be to investigate *peloria*. "By careful examination of its curiosities, one could gain insights into previously unknown, very important truths." He did not yet understand where this theory might lead. Despite his great enthusiasm, Linnaeus stewed in a mix of certainty, doubt, and religious caution . . . for twenty-two years.

During that time, Linnaeus's thinking inched closer to evolutionary ideas. Finally, in 1766, when he revised *Systema Naturae* for his twelfth and final time, with one stroke of his goose-quill pen he deleted the line "nullae species novae" from his definition of the word "species."

PELORIA UPDATE

Linnaeus sent some of the seeds from his *peloria* specimens to Bernard de Jussieu, demonstrator at the Royal Garden in Paris. After seven years of experimenting, Jussieu's colleague Michel Adanson determined that it was not a new species but a *"monstre par excès"*: a monster of excess. It had too many spurs and too many stamens. Over a hundred years later, a plant like this would be described as a mutation.

Linnaeus was not the first to see a plant mutation and Adanson was not the first to identify one. In 1590, a German pharmacist found a malformation of another species in his herb garden, and in 1719, a Frenchman discovered a malformed dog's mercury plant. In 1900, Dutch botanist Hugo de Vries defined the concept of mutation: a change in hereditary genetic material. Linnaeus and his contemporaries were unaware of the existence of genes and chromosomes.

In 1999, British researchers proved that Linnaeus's *peloria* was a plant form caused by a hereditary mutation that occurs naturally in regular toadflax, *Linaria vulgaris*. This mutation is caused when a single gene, the cycloidea gene, which controls the symmetry of the flower, is inactivated.

Mutant *linaria* survive today and are found in Europe as well as the United States. Some of these mutated, or what are now called "peloric," plants have been found in Rhode Island and Pennsylvania.

"No new species," the phrase he wrote in his first edition of *Systema Naturae*, the phrase he had so often repeated to his students, so often written in his books, the phrase that had channeled much of his thinking, he now dropped quietly and without fanfare.

Consider what this decision—this three-word cut—must have meant for him. Although he was not orthodox, he was a religious man. By deleting the phrase "no new species," he must have known that he was opening the door to new ideas, specifically to the rebellious, controversial idea that new species could be created.

A few years later his son, Carl Linnaeus the Younger, also a botanist, told him that some specimens of *linaria* had turned up with both normal and abnormal flowers on the same plant. This would have cast doubt on his conclusions about *peloria*. But Linnaeus wanted to hear nothing more about the plant. He seemed to still feel trapped on the edge of that cliff.

Even after Linnaeus's death in 1778, and more than thirty years after his *peloria* work, a German scientist charged that he had been an atheist. In his diary, however, Linnaeus was clear that his faith in God never wavered, even though it seems that his interpretation of the story of creation had changed. Science historians confirm that his later writings show he eventually came to view species as "the daughters of time"—in other words, that the species could change over time.

That monster of a plant, however, was not the only life form that got Linnaeus into hot water. The animal kingdom brought plenty of conflicts too. One animal in particular was a problem: the human.

9

<><><><><><><><><><><><><><><><><><><><><><><><><><><><><><><><>

HUMAN
VS. ANIMAL

If I were to call man an ape or vice versa, I should
bring down all the theologians on my head.

—CARL LINNAEUS, LETTER TO JOHANN GEORG GMELIN,
  JANUARY 14, 1747

In 1735, Carl Linnaeus had become the first naturalist to classify humans in the same order as apes and monkeys. It was a
move that angered critics and clergymen, who sharpened their
quill pens to strike back.

That year, while living in Holland, Linnaeus came face to face
with live apes and monkeys for the first time. Their similarities
to humans were hard to miss—their teeth, hands, the nails on
their fingers and toes, for instance.

At the time, Linnaeus was studying the banana and other
exotic plants on George Clifford's country estate. The Dutch East
India Company director also kept a private zoo of tigers, wild
dogs, swine, parrots, and monkeys. Sometimes when Linnaeus
traveled to Amsterdam, he visited a world-famous tavern called

This advertisement for Blue John's tavern was an imaginative interpretation. Patrons did sit at outside tables, but the animals did not roam freely in the courtyard for obvious reasons. Lions were kept inside the inn in flimsy wooden enclosures; to see them cost extra.

Blue John's. The tavern was located near the wharf where the Dutch East and West India Companies owned stables and warehouses. Sailors made a little extra income by selling to Blue John natural marvels they'd brought from other countries. The innkeeper displayed wax figures of humans and a large menagerie of exotic animals for customers to admire or, if they could afford the high prices, to buy. The inn sold to royalty and wealthy collectors all over Europe. But for the price of a tankard of ale, a person of modest means, like Linnaeus, could sit at a table for hours and watch animals in the courtyard cages, as long as he kept buying drinks.

At Blue John's, Linnaeus saw porcupines and civet cats. There were tame ostriches as tall as horses, parrots that spoke Dutch better than he did, anteaters and lions, to name a few. For a young man wanting to compare species, this was the place to be. Assembled before him were animals from Southeast Asia and the Dutch colonies in the West Indies, South America and West Africa. This was armchair travel at its best: the excitement of field research minus the danger of sea voyages and deadly jungle fevers.

Of all the rare animals, he was most captivated by the monkeys. "There are none so delightful, so strange and different." He described them in a letter to a friend:

> They are more amusing than comedies or clowns. God has made the world a theatre, and it would not be right if the only clowns were human beings and never a member of another species.

He was mesmerized. Linnaeus was hunting for similarities and differences between animals. These would guide him as he created groups of animals and distinguished individual species from the rest. In fact, he had had a burst of insight three years earlier when, by the side of a road in northern Sweden, he found the lower jawbone of a horse. There were six front teeth. Next came two canine teeth, and in the back he counted twelve molars, six on each side.

This accidental find fit with an idea he'd been mulling over. "If I knew how many teeth and of what peculiar form [each animal has], as well as how many udders and where situated," Linnaeus speculated in his trip journal, "I should perhaps be able to contrive a most natural methodical arrangement of quadrupeds [four-footed animals]." Already he was seeing patterns useful for his new system of classifying animals, just as he was finding patterns in the reproductive organs of plants.

◇◇◇

People at the time knew that humans were "natural beings." They accepted Aristotle's two-thousand-year-old idea that "Man is animal." However, they made a distinction: humans were "animal," but they were not "beasts" like lions and tigers and apes.

In the early 1700s, scientists still followed the general idea of the Great Chain of Being. The concept of a ladderlike scheme to organize nature was devised in ancient Greece by Plato, Aristotle's teacher, around 400 BC. Together, the visual ideas of a ladder and a chain brought hierarchy and continuity to the way people viewed nature. At the top were the immortal beings; first came God, then the angels. Below them were all the mortal beings. Of those, man stood highest, on his own separate rung. Beneath him were three rungs for beasts, plants, and rocks. However, between Plato's time and Linnaeus's, natural philosophers had modified the Great Chain. They completely isolated man from the beasts by not classifying him at all. Man had been separated from the rest of nature.

This made no sense to Linnaeus. He saw no scientific reason to separate humans from the rest of the animals. Nature was a whole. Humans were part of that interconnected web of life.

Linnaeus's method made it possible to describe every creature—cat, dog, or human—in the same way. To do that, he chose characteristics that were obvious, that could be seen and compared, such as teeth, feet, and anatomical structure, and behaviors such as how they moved, gave birth, and fed their young.

When complaints came his way, he wrote defensively, "No one is right to be angry with me." After all, he argued, if man was not a stone and not a flower, man must be in the third kingdom—the kingdom of animals. Linnaeus did not tiptoe around what he saw as a fact of nature.

Still, how to define the human species was the big problem. Philosophers had been grappling with this thorny question for thousands of years. What does it mean to be human? Choosing the characteristics to describe humans scientifically was a dilemma for Linnaeus, too. Was it the hairy body, teeth, hands and feet, upright stance? How they moved? How they gave birth to and fed their young? Their ability to speak words? The brain, intelligence, their ability to reason? What characteristics made humans different from the rest of the animal kingdom? And which animals were similar to them? In other words, where did humans belong in the web of life?

Enter the apes.

When Linnaeus was finishing work on his first edition of *Systema Naturae* in 1735, the year he began living in Holland, he was already convinced that humans belonged in the animal kingdom, probably somewhere near the apes and monkeys.

In that book, he sorted the more than five hundred known animals into six broad classes: four-footed animals, birds, amphibians, fish, insects, and worms. Needing a place for humans, he chose the group most similar to us, the quadrupeds: quad-, from the Latin word for "four," and -ped, meaning "foot." This class was used commonly by scientists for other animals. But, humans with four feet? It certainly was not a perfect fit. He rationalized his classification of humans with the four-footed animals by saying that as babies we crawl on all fours. That was a stretch, but other quadruped characteristics did fit, such as having body hair, giving birth to live young, and nursing them.

Next, he divided the four-footed animals into five smaller orders: humanlike animals; predatory wild animals; rodents; beasts of burden; and grazing animals such as cows, deer, and camels.

Then he subdivided each order into genera. The order of humanlike animals, or Anthropomorpha, had three genera: *Homo*, the Latin word for "human"; *Simia*, meaning "ape"; and *Bradypus*, meaning "sloth." (Sloths have pectoral teats; in other words, their nipples are located on their chests, a characteristic they share only with humans and apes.)

Critics bristled at the thought of classifying humans with the other animals. Some objected that it was wrong because humans had "souls" and animals did not. Linnaeus, however, saw things differently:

Theology decrees that man has a soul and that the animals are mere automata mechanica [mechanical robots], but I believe . . . that animals [also] have a soul and that the difference is in its nobility.

Since the soul and its nobility were not visible physical features, they could not be measured in any scientific way. He explained:

I well know what a splendidly great difference there is [between] a man and a [beast] when I look at them from a point of view of morality. . . . but all this belongs to another forum; it behooves me like a cobbler to stick to my last [a shoemaker's form shaped like a person's foot], in my own workshop, and as a naturalist to consider man and his body, for I know scarcely one feature by which man can be distinguished from apes, if it be not that all the apes have a gap between their fangs and their other teeth, which will be shown by the results of further investigation.

Visible physical features and behaviors were, according to Linnaeus, the keys to unlocking nature's God-given order.

German naturalist Jacob Theodor Klein wrote to Linnaeus and offered two practical arguments against his classification. First, he pointed out that man walked on two feet, not four, so he could not be a quadruped. Second, he noted that man was man, not merely "manlike." Of the man–ape–sloth group, only the apes were really like humans. Reasonable points, of course. Linnaeus took them under consideration.

Several years later, in 1754, still contemplating how similar humans and apes were, Linnaeus was thrilled to receive a guenon monkey. Since the death of his raccoon Sjupp in 1747, no other animal in his expanding menagerie influenced him as much as this beautiful monkey from Africa's west coast. She was typical of her kind—black with a white goatee. Linnaeus thought the white crescent moon that fringed her forehead looked like a hairpiece in the latest style. Reminded of the mythical goddess of the hunt and wild animals, who wore a moon-shaped crown, he called her Diana. In 1758 he named her species *Simia diana* (currently *Cercopithecus diana*).

About the size of a cat, Diana had teeth similar to those of humans and other apes. Her favorite foods were rutabaga, turnip, fruits, nuts, almonds, and raisins. She also ate all kinds of greens and vegetables, porridge, eggs, and blood, but never meat.

Diana, a tropical monkey, loved being warm. During the cold Swedish winters, she lived in the medical garden's orangery with its large, bright windows. At night, after the garden boys threw extra logs on the fire, she climbed high in the building. Up there, it was as warm and steamy as a sauna. On the hottest summer days, she escaped the extreme heat by hanging out in the shade of the garden's trees. But on chilly summer nights, she cried out to every passerby for sympathy.

Diana's humanlike ways were a marvel to Linnaeus. She

An engraving of Linnaeus's guenon monkey, Diana, from his 1754 report.

could "grasp, sit, eat, threaten, [and] smile." Her "mild eyes," he said, reflected her gentle temperament. Like a proud father, he even wrote down her first two words: "Grech," her reply when someone shouted at her, and "Hoi!" when she was frightened. Unleashed indoors, she scampered around, toppling chairs and dumping food on the floor, seemingly for fun.

Intrigued by the intelligence displayed by Diana and her kind, Linnaeus told his students that monkeys in the wild took turns watching for tigers so the rest of their group could sleep and that one ape in captivity had learned to play backgammon.

BOTANISKA TRÄDGÅRDEN I UPSALA PÅ LINNÉS TID. Efter en gravyr från 1769.

The botanic garden in Uppsala. In summer, monkeys were chained to tall poles outside where they could sit on platforms below their specially-built houses.

◇◇◇

Meanwhile, scientific knowledge was increasing rapidly. Previously unknown plants and animals were being discovered around the world. Linnaeus's notes reveal something important about him: when new facts came along, he was open to changing his mind. He jotted thoughts, corrections, and additions in the margins of his personal copies of his published books. He used these notes to revise his works for later editions.

His list of known animal species grew from 569 in 1735 to more than four thousand in 1758. By then, it had become even clearer that earlier classifications needed fixing. Therefore, in 1758, when he overhauled *Systema Naturae*, he did a lot more than simply add species. He took the opportunity to make fundamental changes.

Critics and friends had shown him that some terms didn't match their assigned animals. In Paris, the comte de Buffon—

who, like Linnaeus, had a big ego—gleefully pointed out that some of Linnaeus's groups were artificial, not natural, for instance, the one in which he lumped together humans and two-toed sloths. So Linnaeus replaced the order Quadrupedia, or four-footed animals, with a new one he called Mammalia. The number of feet didn't matter anymore. He also got rid of the class Anthropomorpha, or humanlike animals, and created in its place a new class he called Primates, meaning primary or ranked first among the animals. After making those two changes, he shuffled the species between them, like puzzle pieces, to places where they fit.

The sloth joined the order Mammalia, in the class Bruta with the elephants. Another species he moved was the bat. Previously bats had been classified as birds. Linnaeus now called them

A page from Linnaeus's own copy of his 1737 book *Genera Plantarum*, showing lines left blank and filled in with handwritten notes as new information arrived. He kept this copy on his shelf until he was ready to bring out a revised edition in 1742.

Linnaeus's drawing of a bat with big ears and cartoony toes from 1727, when he was in high school. Bats were classified with the predatory animals at that time.

primates, maybe because of what appeared to be finger bones. The year after Linnaeus died, these mammals were separated from the Primates and given their own order, Chiroptera, meaning "hand-winged."

Linnaeus also moved the whale. Scientists had long thought these giant sea creatures were fish. Even though his knowledgeable friend, the late Peter Artedi, may have suspected otherwise, he too had classified them with the fish. No one knows when a sketch of a bottlenose whale was given to Linnaeus, or whether it influenced this change in classification. It depicted a stranded pregnant whale that had died on a beach at Fredrikshald, Norway, in November 1749. The unborn calf was found inside its mother's body connected by an umbilical cord. If the whale hadn't died, Linnaeus understood, she would have given birth to a live whale calf. Scientists were finally ready to accept that whales were mammals.

Another big change guaranteed Linnaeus's place as a pioneer in science history. As he had done with plants five years earlier, he now gave consistent binomials, or two-word names, to every one of those four thousand animal species. We still use many of the names he coined, such as *Elephas maximus* (Asian elephant) and *Canis lupus* (gray wolf).

Linnaeus's name for our species, *Homo sapiens*, meaning "wise human," was not physically descriptive, and his full scientific definition of the species was unusually brief and cryptic: "Know yourself." In this way, Linnaeus invited us to know ourselves as human animals and to understand our place in the natural world. He was also acknowledging that not every

This watercolor sketch of a whale and her unborn calf is one of the earliest images of the species later determined to be a bottlenose whale. Painted by an unknown artist, it still hangs over the door of Linnaeus's bedroom at Hammarby.

man is wise (*sapiens*), but should strive to achieve *sapientia*, the virtue of wisdom. He was convinced that our ability to reason and show wisdom distinguished our species from apes and any other "cousins of man." Perhaps he hoped this would satisfy the theologians as well as his own religious concerns.

Along with the human species, Linnaeus placed the *Simia*, the apes and monkeys, in the class Primates. This innovation was daring and controversial because it rejected both the old hierarchy of the Chain of Being and the prevailing view of man as being separate and apart from the other animals. What did he really mean by this change? He was saying that apes and humans were different species, but physically similar—but he was not saying that humans and apes were "related" to each other. As far as Linnaeus knew, as far as anyone knew at the time, that was impossible.

Nonetheless, Linnaeus was still under fire. Swiss naturalist Albrecht von Haller mocked him for arrogantly thinking himself "a second Adam." Welsh zoologist Thomas Pennant, a correspondent who generally admired Linnaeus's botanical work, rejected his classification of man. "My vanity would not suffer me to rank mankind with apes, monkeys, maucaucos [lemurs], and bats," he admitted in a letter.

Another critic took aim from Rome. Just as the tenth edition of *Systema Naturae* was published in 1758, Pope Clement XIII began his reign as leader of the worldwide Catholic Church. Clement ordered artists to apply paper fig leaves to the Vatican's "indecent" classical statues and paint over nudes on the Sistine Chapel frescoes—and he forbade the use of Linnaeus's books in the Vatican's gardens. It is possible that he had been offended by terminology in Linnaeus's so-called "sexual system" of plants. Or he may have seen the classification of man with the apes as an attack on the prevailing biblical view. Whatever Pope Clement's reason was for the ban, the next pope lifted it in 1773 and even fired the director of Rome's botanical garden for not knowing the Linnaean system.

◇◇◇

Linnaeus assumed that there must be "cousins of man" somewhere in the world. He imagined that these separate living species would be classified in between humans and apes. In searching for other human species, the "cousins," Linnaeus carefully followed the principles of science, as he understood them. "Nature does not proceed by leaps," he often told his students. He wrote:

> The absence of things not yet discovered has acted as a cause of the deficiencies of the natural method; but the acquisition of knowledge of more things will make it perfect; for nature makes no leaps.

Linnaeus thought that there would be more species to discover in the gaps, in both the animal kingdom and the plant kingdom.

When discussing plants, for example, he explained that groups of plants were like islands in a sea. One student drew this island map from his class notes. The circles were islands. They represented orders of plants. The bigger the circle, the more genera it contained. A circle's location on the map showed how close, or similar, it was to other groups of plants, or how remote. Along the

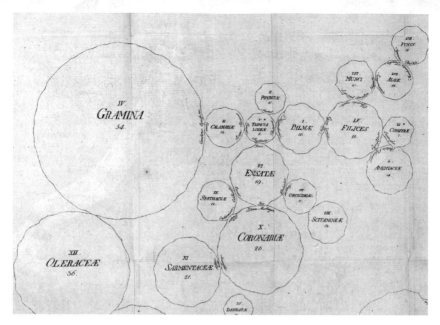

A "genealogical/geographical map" of plants drawn by one of Linnaeus's students from his class notes. Where some circles touched, he penned names of genera with traits similar to plants in the order next door. For instance, palms (*Palmae*) were linked with ferns (*Filices*). In this part of his drawing, the order of grasses (*Gramina*) is the largest and contains the most genera.

inside edges of neighboring circles, the student wrote the names of plants with similar closely related features, like palms and ferns.

However, Linnaeus and his students didn't believe that natural orders were "related" to each other by heredity. To Linnaeus, the white space—the "ocean" between the "islands"—represented gaps in his knowledge. Any missing species had simply not been found yet.

In the animal world, in particular, Linnaeus recognized that limited knowledge made it difficult to find the in-between species. He theorized that

. . . there are somewhere apes which are less hairy than man, erect in position, going just like him [man] on two feet, and recalling the human species by the use they make of their hands and feet, to such an extent, that the less educated travellers have given them out as a kind of man.

In the 1700s, Europeans knew little about the animals and people in far-off regions of the world. Linnaeus had to make use of the information available to him—colleagues' letters, publications and reports of sailors and travelers. He waded through all their claims to judge whether they were true or false. Some stories turned out to be secondhand tales, others were wild exaggerations

This illustration was published in England in Edward Tyson's *The Anatomy of a Pygmie*. People debated whether this creature was a primitive sort of human and watched animals in captivity for signs of civility, such as table manners.

VARIATIONS

Since Linnaeus had already divided some animal and plant species into subcategories called "varieties," in 1758 he followed the pattern with humans. He identified four variations, which were geographically based: Americanus, Afer (meaning from Africa), Europaeus, and Asiaticus. A fifth variety, Monstrosus, was a catchall group for everything he was unsure of. This was the first serious scientific attempt to subdivide the human species.

In order to write the full scientific descriptions, however, he relied on the ancient theory of humors: red blood, white phlegm, yellow bile, and black bile. This provided an observable characteristic—color. The result was a racist and misguided linking of continent, skin color, and temperament. Especially problematic was the linking of color to temperament. These descriptions are offensive stereotypes and are not used today.

meant to impress the folks back home. Some unreliable reports confused chimpanzees, orangutans, baboons, and gibbons with one another and even with humans.

Linnaeus was led astray by travelers claiming to have seen humans who lived in caves and came out only at night. He named them *Homo troglodytes*, meaning cave-dweller, but we know now that these light-skinned children of dark-skinned parents were afflicted with a rare inherited disorder called albinism. Their pure white skin was easily sunburned, and their eyes were extremely sensitive to daylight.

He also was misled by a 1658 report by Jacob Bontius, physician to the Dutch settlement on the island of Java. Bontius

This is how he organized humans in 1735:

KINGDOM	ORDER	CLASS	GENUS	SPECIES	VARIETY
Animalia	Quadrupedia (four-footed)	Anthropo-morpha (humanlike)	1. *Homo* (human)	*sapiens* (wise)	
			2. *Simia* (ape)		
			3. *Bradypus* (sloth)		

And this was how he reorganized us in 1758:

Animalia	Mammalia (mammals)	Primates (primary)	1. *Homo* (human)	*sapiens* (wise)	1. Americanus 2. Europaeus 3. Asiaticus 4. Africanus 5. Monstrosus
				troglodytes (cave-dwelling)	
			2. *Simia*		
			3. *Lemur*		
			4.*Vespertilio* (bat)		

All "varieties" of humans were one species: *Homo sapiens.*

◇◇

described a live animal brought from Borneo. Called "ourang-outang" locally, Bontius gave it a Latin name, *Homo sylvestris,* meaning "man of the forest."

In 1699, British physician Edward Tyson reused the name *Homo sylvestris* for another animal, even though he realized it was probably different from the one Bontius described. Tyson, dissecting the animal, compared its anatomy with those of the ape and the human and found it had more in common with the human than the ape, especially when it came to the brain. He concluded it was neither human nor ape, but something in between. People debated whether the creature was a primitive sort of human and watched for signs of civility, such as table manners. Not until 1929 was this species correctly identified as the pygmy chimpanzee.

Linnaeus also named a species of tailed man, *Homo caudatus*, based on a confused sailor's misinterpretation of ceremonial clothing made of bark worn by people from the Nicobar Islands in the eastern Indian Ocean.

Although Linnaeus turned out to be wrong about *troglodytes*, *sylvestris*, and *caudatus*, scientists now know that other human species did exist but long ago became extinct. Since the nineteenth century, remains of more than a dozen extinct species of primitive or early-modern human ancestors have been found around the world. For example, in 2013, fossil remains of *Homo naledi* were discovered in South Africa. His bones suggest that he was a toolmaker who also climbed trees. Even though *Homo naledi* was related to our species, he was not our direct ancestor. However, scientists recently discovered in today's human genome DNA from another "cousin" who lived in Siberia 50,000 years ago—proof that *Homo neanderthalensis* was our direct ancestor.

◇◇◇

While Linnaeus taught new generations of students and worked on revising his "System of Nature," the menagerie in the university's botanic garden grew. Like the people of the province where he grew up, Linnaeus was thrifty. He was not inclined to purchase animals. Those he had were given as gifts by his traveling students, admirers around the world, and sea captains of the Swedish East India Company. Many came from the Swedish king and queen.

Raising animals was nothing new to Linnaeus. When he was a child, his father kept domesticated pigeons, horses, cows, and sheep. His brother Samuel, now a pastor, kept honeybees. As a university student, Carl had hung branches around his room, where some thirty species of birds, including larks and sparrows, found places to perch or nest. It is not known how his landlady felt about his feathered roommates.

Professor Linnaeus continued to observe the varying intelligence, temperaments, behaviors, and cleverness among many different species right there in Uppsala. Several monkeys—a Barbary macaque, a marmoset, a white-headed capuchin, and a tufted capuchin, as well as his favorite, the guenon monkey Diana—chattered from their special houses in the garden. North American raccoons, a guinea pig, a South American coati, a rodent called an agouti, and, from Madagascar, several kinds of lemurs—black and ring-tailed lemurs and a mongoose—roamed the flowerbeds or lived in the animal house by the orangery. Goldfish from China swam in a barrel, while parrots—a scarlet macaw, a blue-fronted amazon, and an African grey—squawked, whistled, and shrieked from the trees.

Some animals even lived with the family in their big yellow house. Sara Lisa had a full, busy household and a farm to oversee, five children to raise, live-in students to care for, other students tramping in and out for lectures, plus several servants and farmhands to supervise. She was often asked by the university to host parties. It was good that she was a capable organizer, but being married to Linnaeus was probably challenging. For instance, one evening he and a professor who'd arrived early to a party launched into a spirited debate. To clarify his point, Linnaeus grabbed a stick of wood char from the kitchen fire and wrote notes all over the clean kitchen floor.

Animal antics added to the already exuberant household. The African grey parrot was a talented mimic. One day an old gardener, known for blowing his nose loudly before work, entered the garden, and the parrot squawked a command, "Blow your nose!"

Occasionally a student would knock on the professor's office door. "Step in!" came the reply. The student would be baffled to find the room empty except for the parrot.

During the family's meals, the bird often sat on Linnaeus's shoulder waiting for handouts. If lunch was late, the parrot reminded him, "Twelve o'clock, Mr. Carl!"

Elsewhere, a clever little monkey named Grinn was raising a ruckus at the royal court. With nimble fingers, the monkey, who was no bigger than a kitten, unfastened and stole the silver buckles from everyone's shoes. The queen had had enough monkey trouble. She banished the cotton-top tamarin, along with his formal portrait, sending them as a "gift" to the only person she knew who would be excited to take him in. Professor

Grinn was portrayed in oil on canvas by Gustav Hesselius for the king and queen. The peanut shell provides a size comparison.

Linnaeus welcomed the exiled New World monkey into his noisy menagerie.

◇◇◇

In addition to the scientific hustle and bustle of Linnaeus's house, his students benefited from the systems and tools he was developing. These made thinking about the natural world clearer, easier, faster. The next generation of scientists would build its own revolutionary ideas on the foundations that Linnaeus and his predecessors laid. They explored ideas that Linnaeus probably never imagined.

In 1809, French taxonomist Jean-Baptiste Lamarck proposed a radical theory: that human beings actually had transformed, or evolved, from apes. Lamarck's contemporary, Georges Cuvier, compared living animals with fossils and confirmed that entire species could die out, proving that extinction was a fact. Gone was the idea of a fixed number of unchanging species.

In the 1850s, British naturalist Charles Darwin looked back at the scientists who preceded him. He commented in a letter to the author of a new book about Aristotle, "Linnaeus and Cuvier have been my two gods, though in different ways, but they were mere school-boys compared to old Aristotle." Darwin, whose grandfather, Erasmus Darwin, had been a fan of Linnaeus, admired these three—Linnaeus, Cuvier, and Aristotle—for their ability to organize massive amounts of information so that it could be understood. Linnaeus was not only a precursor to Darwin, but a hero.

In 1872, Darwin wrote a letter to a French paleontologist:

I cannot at present give up my belief in the close relationship of Man to the higher Simiae [apes] . . . for I cannot believe that such resemblances can be due to any cause except close blood-relationship. That man is closely allied to the higher Simiae is shewn [sic] by the classification of Linnaeus, who was so good a judge of affinity.

In his groundbreaking 1859 book, *On the Origin of Species*, Darwin wrote, "Expressions such as that famous one by Linnaeus . . . that the characters do not make the genus, but that the genus gives the characters, seem to imply that some deeper bond is included in our classification than mere resemblance."

The monkeys clowning around at Blue John's, Diana's mild eyes, the buckle-stealing rascal Grinn, and even the African grey parrot's squawky talk all showed Linnaeus examples of animal intelligence, some surprisingly human.

His view of man's place in the animal kingdom did not follow Plato's Great Chain, but it was not quite Darwin's evolutionary thinking either. Scientific thought was inching forward. In classifying the apes near the humans, in recognizing the balance of nature and the battle for survival (the "war of all against all"), and in acknowledging that species could change (species are the work of time), Linnaeus became part of the bridge that guided science into the future.

Linnaeus's legacy would be cemented by the next generation. A new wave of young scientists, brilliant and brave, went out to explore the world.

10

STUDENT EXPLORERS

A professor can never better distinguish himself in his work than by encouraging a clever pupil, for the true discoverers are among them, as comets amongst the stars.

—CARL LINNAEUS, LETTER TO THE ROYAL SWEDISH
ACADEMY OF SCIENCES REQUESTING A SCHOLARSHIP
FOR DANIEL ROLANDER, MARCH 12, 1752

Floorboards creaked at dawn across Uppsala as students and townies yawned and rolled out of bed. Every Wednesday or Saturday from April to July, they pulled on the required uniform—comfortable short jackets, baggy white sailor pants, broad-brimmed hats—grabbed their gear and headed out. They were about to embark on an exhilarating twelve-hour nature hike, led by the best naturalist in all of Sweden.

Promptly at 7 a.m., the group—a couple hundred young men of various nationalities, and rarely a few women—gathered at a tollgate where the road led out into the countryside. Excitement crackled through the crowd.

Professor Carl Linnaeus organized his "army of botanists" into companies, military style. The general, Linnaeus of course, appointed captains and second lieutenants. Also chosen were shooters to kill birds for close examination, a secretary to record results, and a law enforcer to keep discipline.

The troops came armed with field equipment, including butterfly nets, pins, pocket knives, collapsible microscopes, magnifying glasses, paper, and black lead for writing notes. Most carried a vasculum, a long copper cylinder which opened lengthwise, to keep plant specimens fresh until evening.

Linnaeus varied the experience by alternating among eight routes with different habitats. At stops along the way, he sent the hikers off to explore. In meadows and marshes, they collected plants, insects, stones, reptiles, fish and "little birds that are shot." When someone made a spectacular find, a bugle was blown to call the group together. Every half hour they gathered so that Linnaeus could guide them in identifying their specimens. He discussed the best ones in detail, yet had something to say about even the least significant finds. Often he added humorous stories, like the one about the German clergyman Pastor Hieronymus Bock who, while writing a book about plants in the 1500s, found one in a field that he didn't recognize. He asked a student visiting from Sweden if he knew its name. The boy answered in Swedish, *"Knäfvelen vet,"* meaning "the devil knows." Thinking the boy had told him the plant's name, the pastor wrote down what he heard: "Knavel." Linnaeus had high standards for plant names—no swear words allowed, including this botched spelling of an old Swedish word for "devil." Linnaeus changed the name to *Scleranthus annuus*, but his students would always remember the uninteresting-looking weed by its story.

At two o'clock, the hungry group stopped for lunch, sometimes at the invitation of one of Linnaeus's botanical friends, a local baron whose estate was on the route, or later at one of Linnaeus's farm cottages in Hammarby and Sävja. Johan Christian Fabricius, a Danish student, described the typical picnic scene:

> A table was spread for twenty, provided with fruit and syllabubs [a sweet, foamy milk drink], and those who had found the rarest plants sat with the Master at this table; the rest ate standing up, hoping one day to enjoy the honour all envied and which was enough to stimulate the most lively competition among these young rivals.

At 9 p.m., after an especially long hike, the boisterous, ragtag bunch marched back into Uppsala shouting, "Vivat Linnaeus!" Long live Linnaeus! Fabricius wrote, "They returned into the town with Flowers in their hats, and with Kettle-Drums and Hunting Horns followed their leader to the Garden through the entire Town."

On their way back, some students did last-minute botanizing in professors' hop gardens and plucked cabbages from fenced garden patches owned by city officials. Some even climbed onto the low "house roofs in Uppsala, which are covered with green growing sods of turf," to add to their plant collections. Needless to say, the residents and other professors did not appreciate the noisy nighttime botanical invasions or boys climbing on their roofs.

Linnaeus already was seen as self-important and egotistical among professors whose own classes were much less popular. Some years later, the secretary of the Royal Swedish Academy of Sciences would write in a letter that everybody valued Linnaeus, but "hardly anyone loves him, not even here." At one point in 1748, the university forced Linnaeus to stop the rambunctious field trips, at least temporarily.

◇◇◇

Botanical excursions were only one way that Linnaeus prepared his students to go out on their own and work independently. His demonstrations in the medical garden and longer expeditions with small groups of student assistants to explore other regions of Sweden also gave them firsthand experience.

Back at the university, students often packed Linnaeus's lectures and private tutoring sessions. Unlike many professors who droned on as they read their written lectures, Linnaeus was an enthusiastic teacher, animated and funny. He lectured mostly from memory. His teaching methods were nothing like those he'd suffered as a boy, when schoolmasters beat students for giving wrong answers or misbehaving. Those experiences inspired him to be a different kind of teacher. Instead, he won over his students by caring about them—he invited students to dinner, hired some as live-in tutors for his son, helped them secure financial grants. He encouraged them and shared with them his obvious excitement about natural science.

One student recalled that Linnaeus's voice was not strong or pleasant, and sometimes he slipped into the heavy dialect of

Småland, the southern province where he grew up. Knowing that Latin when spoken in his regional accent could be hard for foreign students to understand, Linnaeus often began private lectures with an apology. Another student, who later became a medical professor himself, marveled that Linnaeus "never failed to captivate his audiences. He knew how to emphasize certain words in his short sentences so expressively that no one could possibly fail to be convinced by his argument." In addition to persuasiveness, the student said:

> . . . he had the advantage of a clear mind and incomparable memory, so that he could deliver a long oration or a lecture from a few notes scribbled on a scrap of paper . . . which he would hold between his fingers, marking with his thumb the point he had reached.

Another student noted the professor's ability to move his listeners:

> If Linnaeus spoke of the power and majesty of the Creator, reverence and wonder showed on every face; . . . on the rules of diet, he often made his students roar with laughter by his descriptions of the follies of fashion, using a joke and a light touch to teach a valuable lesson about the care and preservation of health.

Students flocked to Uppsala to study the revolutionary new botanical system with the man who had created it. He was a magnet. He drew students from across the Scandinavian peninsula and from Denmark, Finland, England, Germany,

Spain, Italy, Russia, Switzerland, and even South Africa. They were various ages, some as young as nine but most between twenty-five and thirty-five years old. They came from families rich and poor. Sons of a wealthy nobleman from Russia were sent by the tsar to learn the Linnaean system, but many of his students were penniless sons of rural Swedish clergymen, as he had been.

During Linnaeus's thirty-five years as a professor, he taught hundreds of students. Most became physicians. Some made their careers as surgeons and veterinarians, others botanists and naturalists, as well as mine inspectors, government officials, and clergymen. Twenty-three became professors teaching at various European universities. But seventeen of his best and bravest students became explorers. Although he never used the word in print, informally Linnaeus called those traveling disciples his "apostles."

◇◇◇

Between 1745 and 1799, the "apostles" took part in important scientific expeditions to distant regions of the world. They had no idea whether they'd make it back alive; in fact, several didn't.

How did the dream of one man propel so many others to take such risks? Why did these young people choose to go on such dangerous journeys into the unknown?

Like their professor, they were passionate about the world's plants and animals. The natural world was not only their classroom, it was their life's work. They thrilled at its wonders. They longed to solve its mysteries. They too saw the urgent need for taking stock of all the world's species. They believed in their professor's work and wanted to contribute. But they were individuals, and their reasons weren't only idealistic; they also needed to launch their careers.

Why did Linnaeus encourage them to go? For his part, Linnaeus had had enough roughing it in Sápmi to last him a lifetime. He liked the comforts of home and family. Still, he needed data to accomplish the task that he and Peter Artedi had begun back when they were students. These rugged young explorers could assist him in two ways: by discovering new species—the data—to help complete his global list, and also by spreading enthusiasm for his revolutionary system.

What part did Linnaeus play in the travel of these young naturalists? He suggested places to explore. He wangled money for their trips through grants from the Royal Swedish Academy of Sciences, wealthy patrons, and governments. He leaned on his carefully cultivated global network of influential botanists, monarchs, and sea captains to help them find paying jobs as ship's doctors, surgeons, chaplains, or naturalists on expeditions and as tutors of the children of men stationed at colonial outposts. For some of his students, he was able to secure promises of professorial posts at universities or botanical gardens for their return.

Later Linnaeus would depict this as a grand campaign, planned and directed from "central command" in Uppsala. But in fact, these former students were now adults. They were well-trained scientists, taught by the best. They chose to venture out in the name of science. They were heavily inspired, of course, by their charismatic teacher, but he didn't "send" them. He was the persuader-in-chief.

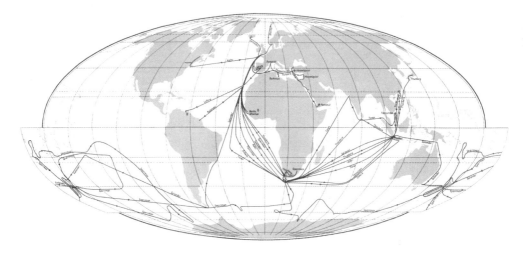

The sea routes of some of Linnaeus's student "apostles" traced on a map of the globe.

These explorations had a discouraging start. In 1746, Linnaeus's first "apostle," Christopher Tärnström, died of a tropical fever on an island near Vietnam in the South China Sea. He was thirty-five years old and left behind a family back in Sweden, two daughters and a devastated wife who blamed Linnaeus. The death shook Linnaeus deeply. From then on, he encouraged travel only among strong young bachelors who could sleep as well "on the hardest bench as on the softest bed, but to find a little plant or moss the longest road wouldn't be too long."

The travelers were sometimes given direction by their paying sponsors or employers, and by Linnaeus—lists of plants, animals, and minerals to look for on particular continents and protocols for preparing and packing specimens for shipment back to Uppsala. Seeds were folded into paper packets.

Acorns, wrapped individually and pressed into a box filled with soft wax, would keep for a year. A plant's root ball could be shipped if first moistened and tied into an ox bladder. Insects were packed in vials. Small animals were preserved in jars of alcohol or in boxes of fine wood shavings called excelsior. Even when perfectly wrapped, specimens were often lost in transit to insects, rats, dampness, and mold, and even washed overboard by heavy seas.

Over a span of fifty years, nearly twenty of Linnaeus's former students traveled to North and South America, Africa, Asia, Australia, and islands in the tropical Pacific Ocean, today called Oceania. Some of their trips lasted only a few months; others took as long as ten years. Their journals, filled with stories of hardship, adventure, and scientific discovery, were as varied as the students who wrote them. Linnaeus urged them to write about science in a readable style—to "imitate nature in such a way that anyone reading the description may feel as though they had the objects in front of their eyes."

They used Linnaeus's contacts and made new ones of their own. They sweated in the heat of tropical jungles. They froze on the polar ice caps. They crawled through thickets and portaged along roaring rivers. They were building careers. They were the next generation of scientists.

◇◇◇

The stories of seven—Pehr Kalm, Daniel Solander, Pehr Löfling, Daniel Rolander, Peter Forsskål, Anders Sparrman, and Carl Peter Thunberg—stood out.

On the globe that sat in Linnaeus's study, the 60th parallel was of particular interest. It circled through Uppsala, through Scotland, Canada, Alaska, and Russia's Kamchatka Peninsula. Linnaeus was convinced that lands at the same latitude around the world had the same climate. If this was correct, plants thriving in parts of all those countries would also grow in Sweden. To test his theory, in 1748, he urged his next "apostle," Pehr Kalm, to go to North America.

Kalm's mission was to collect North American plants that could survive the harsh Swedish climate—chestnut and other nut trees, red and white cedar, sassafras, sugar maples, wild rice, maize, bay myrtle for making candles, potatoes, and wild grapes. Plus, he was to send back shipments of red mulberry, a tree whose leaves were the preferred food of silkworms. The mulberry was expected to launch a silk industry in Sweden. As Linnaeus had done in Sápmi, Kalm also planned to study any plants eaten or used as medicine by the people who lived there. All seeds were to be collected in the most northerly, coldest part of each plant's range.

Kalm arrived in Philadelphia in September 1748. Along the city's riverfront, a jagged row of sixty wooden wharves with countless masts and sails, like the ocean's laundry hung to dry, sprawled a mile in either direction. Kalm stepped from his ship, the *Mary Gally*, onto the wharf and made his way along cobbled streets to the home of Benjamin Franklin. This distinguished man of science was known to Professor Linnaeus through mutual friends in England.

Franklin received the young man graciously, offering advice, a tour of the city, a place to live—and, most importantly, the loan of books. All winter Kalm read books from Franklin's library to help in his research of American plants. Needing a place quieter than Franklin's hectic household to concentrate on his work, he rented a room in a village called Raccoon in what is now Swedesboro in southern New Jersey. Most residents there were descendants of Swedish colonists. The economical landlord kept Kalm's room so cold that he had to tuck his inkstand in his pocket or warm it on the hearth to keep his pen from freezing. Luckily, Franklin loaned him a wood-burning stove.

In June 1750, Kalm began his trek north then west. Travel was tough. He and his guides portaged along the Hudson River around rapids and waterfalls until they reached one so large they abandoned the canoe and made their way through fifty miles of dense forest. Sometimes they crawled on hands and knees through snake-infested woods and tangles of thorny vines. During the day they sweltered. At night the deafening whine of crickets and cicadas, along with the bites and buzzing of mosquitoes and gnats, kept them awake. Tree branches groaned and snapped above them, sometimes crashing to the ground under the weight of thousands of roosting passenger pigeons.

Kalm pressed plants and described them in detail, even those that seemed to be no particular value. He explained:

> I often hear myself reproached when I gather most plants: "He who has nothing else to do must run to and fro and gather moss and more moss for what purpose?" I have found in my travels that the plant most neglected may prove to be the

most useful. I have learned that man at first may consider a plant or an insect as a mere curiosity, a nuisance and a trifle in nature. However, when the uses of this new thing are understood, it cannot be too highly valued.

The practical-minded Kalm was right in step with one of his professor's central themes: commercial usefulness. Botanical explorers were expected to bring back plants that could be cultivated in Sweden and would boost the country's struggling economy by avoiding the financial drain caused by expensive imports.

Kalm also had a long-range view. He complained about the colonists' destruction of forests and whole bird populations, saying, "Hardly could we in Sweden and Finland treat our valuable forests with more hostility than is happening here: they look only to immediate profits, and never even dream about the future."

Like Linnaeus's Arctic journal, Kalm's diary recorded experiences and details about the environment and stories of colonial life in North America. All this, he hoped, would be valuable when he began his promised job teaching at a university in Finland.

Kalm was anxious to see what was said to be a spectacular waterfall. A Franciscan missionary claimed it was 600 feet tall. Kalm and a French acquaintance calculated it more accurately at 160 feet, still an impressive height. An excerpt of his description of Niagara Falls, published by Benjamin Franklin in his *Pennsylvania Gazette* in September 1750, conveys his excitement:

On both sides of this island runs all the water that comes from the Lakes of Canada, [namely] Lake Superior, Lake Michigan, Lake Huron, and Lake Erie, which you know are rather small seas than lakes. . . . When all this water comes to the very fall, there it throws itself down perpendicular! The hair will rise and stand upright on your head, when you see this! I cannot with words express how amazing this is! You cannot see it without being quite terrified; to behold so vast a quantity of water falling headlong from so surprizing [sic] a height!

After more than two years in North America, Kalm returned to the port of Stockholm. Linnaeus wrote to a friend, "Take fire-brands and throw them after Professor Kalm that he may come without delay to Uppsala." But he could not wait: impatient and hurting from a crippling episode of gout, he boarded a boat to Stockholm to meet his student.

Kalm shared his huge collections with his former professor. Even though tensions between French and English colonists in the lead-up to the French and Indian Wars had kept him from traveling as far north into Canada as Linnaeus had hoped, Kalm did bring back hundreds of pressed plants and seeds of species that might survive the cold Swedish climate, including an early-ripening maize, pumpkin, cotton, beans, watermelon, the sugar maple, and three species of walnut trees. Kalm also described an orange dye made from sassafras bark, a blue dye made from red maple, and native sweet potatoes that "almost melt in the mouth."

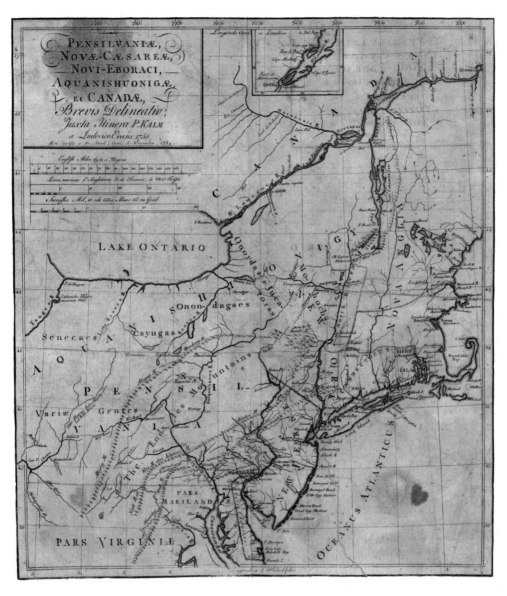

Cartographer Lewis Evans made this map expressly for Pehr Kalm's trip north in 1750. It shows his route from Raccoon, New Jersey, his home base for exploring eastern North America, to Albany and on to Canada. Evans labeled Raccoon, south of Philadelphia, by its church, "T. Suec-icum," meaning "Swedish temple."

Benjamin Franklin praised him: "Our Friend Mr. Kalm, goes home in this Ship, with a great Cargo of Curious Things. I love the Man, and admire his indefatigable Industry." But Kalm, consumed by botanical work and a new job at a university in Finland, unfortunately neglected some basic courtesies: acknowledgments and letters of thanks. Franklin did not forget. Even years later, in 1773 during the hectic days before the Revolution, he wrote, "Kalm's Account of what he learned in America is full of idle Stories, which he pick'd up among ignorant People, and either forgetting of whom he had them, or willing to give them some Authenticity, he has ascrib'd them to Persons of Reputation. . . . It is dangerous conversing with these Strangers that keep Journals."

Despite these blunders, Pehr Kalm was the first trained scientist to comprehensively study the natural history of northeastern America. He brought home to Scandinavia 150 live perennial plants and trees and described at least sixty plant species that were new to science. Other curiosities included a hummingbird's nest, a live opossum, a turtle, three guinea pigs, and, preserved in alcohol, a praying mantis, a star-nosed mole, more turtles, and snakes. The grateful Linnaeus named several plants for Kalm, including the mountain laurel, *Kalmia latifolia*, today the official state flower of both Pennsylvania and Connecticut.

Linnaeus tried and failed to establish tea plants in Sweden. He thought they could be adapted to the colder climate. He imagined cinnamon groves growing in Sápmi and wild Canadian rice in the lakes of Finland. However, many attempts at same-latitude-same-climate transplants were doomed to fail.

Linnaeus's theory that plants could be successfully transplanted from one place on the same latitude to another had a flaw: latitude was not the only influence on climate. Ocean currents and soil types also affect climate and growing zones. A half century later, the German naturalist Alexander von Humboldt would gather temperature records kept by observers in different parts of the world. For North America, he used temperatures recorded by Pehr Kalm with a thermometer that Linnaeus had given him for the trip—one of the first redesigned Celsius thermometers. Humboldt drew lines on a map connecting points of equal temperature. These lines, called isothermals, crossed through the latitude lines, swooping above and below them. One of the causes was the warming effect of the Gulf Stream on

Pehr Kalm was the first scientist to describe Niagara Falls. This engraving ran in London's *Gentleman's Magazine* in 1751. In the center is a ladder of linden bark, made by members of the Six Nations confederacy.

the climates of Europe and coastal North America, observed by Franklin and others.

◇◇◇

Another rising star in Linnaeus's galaxy of students was the friendly and outgoing Daniel Solander, his favorite. They had worked side by side cataloging the royal natural history collections. After pressure from his English friends to send one of his best students to help catalog their collections, Linnaeus suggested that Solander travel briefly to England in 1759. The professor expected that one day this promising young man would be his successor—the next botany professor at Uppsala. He also thought that Solander would marry his daughter. So did Solander. He wrote often from London inquiring about seventeen-year-old Lisa Stina and calling her his "sweetest mademoiselle."

But when, against his former professor's advice, Solander declined an important botanical job in Russia and accepted a permanent post at the newly formed British Museum in London, things changed. Five years later, Solander was still in England, and Lisa Stina had married someone else. The circumstances are unknown. Had Lisa Stina ever been in love with Solander? Had Solander's obsessive passion for plants—like professor, like student—kept him in London too long?

Whatever the cause, Daniel Solander was on the ship *Endeavour* when Captain James Cook sailed it out of Plymouth harbor in the south of England in 1768 on a dangerous three-year circumnavigation of the globe. Cook's main goal was to position the ship near Tahiti in the south Pacific as the planet Venus passed in front of the sun. Astronomers onboard were to calculate the distance from the Earth to the Sun.

Cook's voyages were hardly luxury cruises. Sailors were plagued with scurvy and dysentery. Many died from diseases including malaria and yellow fever. While mapping the coast-

"The Simpling Macaroni": a London cartoon from 1772 mocked Daniel Solander. "Simpling" was the collecting and studying of simples, or herbal medicines with only one plant ingredient. Young travelers were often derided as "macaronis" for their fashionable attire, mannerisms, love of Italian food, and rustic lifestyle.

lines of New Zealand and Australia, the *Endeavour* ran aground on shoals off the Great Barrier Reef. It took seven weeks to repair the badly damaged hull. However, seven weeks on land was a botanist's dream—uninterrupted time for plant hunting. It was so productive that Cook later named the place of their first Australian landfall Botany Bay, after the ship's three botanists.

In his last letter to Linnaeus in 1768 from the *Endeavour*, then anchored off Rio de Janeiro, Solander concluded with greetings to Linnaeus's family and to "your eldest daughter, whom I had hoped would make me happy."

All we know is that Lisa Stina landed in an unhappy marriage to an abusive, unfaithful husband, and Solander never married. Still separated by the North Sea and the British Channel, Lisa Stina died in April 1782 and, in a final twist of fate, Solander died four weeks later.

A tropical American plant genus, *Solandra*, and a few Australian plant species are named for him.

◇◇◇

Another traveling "apostle" was Pehr Löfling. He was the teenager who chased hungry goats in Linnaeus's agriculture survey in 1748. Five years later, the Spanish ambassador told Linnaeus

OPPOSITE: An evergreen shrub found in Australia by botanists aboard the *Endeavour* and sketched by one of them, Sydney Parkinson. Carl Linnaeus the Younger named it *Banksia serrata* in 1782 to honor Joseph Banks, Solander's friend and the chief botanist onboard.

that his country was outfitting an expedition to the Amazon River in South America. They intended to survey the boundary and the natural resources of the colony of New Andalusia, today known as Venezuela. Linnaeus recommended Löfling, one of his most brilliant students.

Löfling jumped at the chance. However, unlike Pehr Kalm, who considered commercial usefulness his main purpose, Löfling had a different motivation. He told Linnaeus up front, "Economy is more of an obligation to me." What really excited him was pure research. He studied nature to understand it better.

In South America, Löfling hunted for plants and closely observed dolphins and manatees. To him, the Amazon freshwater dolphins seemed more like the animals that gave birth to live young than like fishes. He wrote that these "fish breathe through lungs."

Löfling died of malaria in Venezuela, at only twenty-seven years old. Linnaeus mourned his passing and named a plant genus, *Loeflingia*, after him.

◇◇◇

Daniel Rolander headed to the same part of the world in 1754. The Spanish had been hiding a secret there for centuries—a mysterious natural product that the Aztecs had used to produce a vivid red color. It was "the brightest, strongest red the Old World had ever seen." This exotic pigment, called *grana cochinilla* or cochineal (caw-chin-eel), did not fade or wash out. Artists wanted to paint with it, kings and cardinals wanted to wear clothes dyed with it. Only the wealthiest people could afford it.

One day in 1755, a package arrived at the Uppsala University

Illustration of a Mexican cochineal plantation from Sir Hans Sloane's book, *A Voyage to the Islands of Madera, Barbadoes, Nieves, St. Christopher's and Jamaica*—the book that Linnaeus was "traded" for in 1735. In the field, people harvest cochineal beetles, while on the right, a person makes tortillas.

garden. A gardener opened it and panicked when he found a dying cactus. The plant was being devoured by an infestation of tiny beetles. He killed all the insects and tried desperately to revive the dying cactus.

The gardener had no idea that these were rare cochineal beetles, or that Professor Linnaeus had been waiting for months to receive them. Linnaeus wanted to study the live beetles that the Aztecs had ground and dried to make the exotic red dye.

Rolander had finally managed to procure some live beetles

at a Dutch colonial plantation. To keep them alive, he carefully packed them with their preferred food plant, a live prickly pear cactus.

Now all the precious beetles were exterminated, and the professor, who suffered from migraines, wound up with his most severe headache ever.

Rolander had grown up in the same province as Linnaeus and attended Växjö Cathedral School. As a boy, he spent hours alone observing insects, even bringing live wasp nests back to his room to study. When he arrived at Uppsala University, Linnaeus liked him right away. "Greatly impressed" by his enthusiasm and keen observations, Linnaeus encouraged him to submit several papers about insects, including an important one on the deathwatch beetle, to the Royal Swedish Academy of Sciences.

When Pehr Löfling left for South America, Rolander took his place as tutor for Linnaeus's son. For four years, he benefited from daily conversations with his mentor and access to Linnaeus's library, collections, and gardens. The professor was constantly busy writing books, dissertations for students to defend, and letters to international correspondents and his "apostles" away on expeditions.

In 1754, Linnaeus secured a job for Rolander as tutor to the children of a Swede who owned a large plantation in the Dutch colony of Suriname in South America. In a letter requesting a scholarship to fund Rolander's trip, Linnaeus praised him. "As you know," Linnaeus wrote, "for every creative spirit we have a thousand collectors." This young man was a creative spirit.

Once in Suriname, Rolander found the heat unbearable and

the plantation owners' cruel treatment of slaves shocking. He preferred collecting plant and insect specimens to socializing with the colonists and teaching their children. He spent only seven months there.

Twice he faced serious bouts of fever that delayed his travels by months—first in Amsterdam on his way over and then in Germany on his way back home. Finally strong enough but bankrupt, he returned to Sweden in October 1756. When Linnaeus offered free room and board in his home, Rolander turned it down but promised Linnaeus a tropical plant called *Sauvagesia*.

No plant came. Soon Linnaeus realized that, unlike other returning "apostles" who eagerly shared their results, Rolander had no intention of giving him any specimens or even letting him see his herbarium. The reasons remain unclear. Rolander may have felt abandoned and blamed Linnaeus for the journey's difficulties, his suffering and lack of extra financial support during his illnesses. He may have worried that if his Suriname findings were published by Linnaeus first, he would not be able to use them to land a professorship.

Whatever the reason, Linnaeus was furious. He stormed into Rolander's apartment and took the promised *Sauvagesia* specimen. Usually Linnaeus's fiery outbursts dissipated quickly, but not this time. Rolander had created an enemy. Linnaeus never saw Rolander's enormous plant collection from Suriname. He blocked Rolander from getting a job lecturing on plants. It is not known whether Linnaeus prevented the appointment out of spite or because he did not realize that Rolander had become an expert in plants in addition to insects.

As agreed before the trip, Rolander gave a crate of Suriname insects to a benefactor, who was one of the richest Swedes of the time and had contributed money for Rolander's trip. The man, a professional entomologist, lived not far from Linnaeus and allowed his neighbor to study the box of insects. Linnaeus wrote later that he "made me a present of every one of them." As a result, the tenth edition of *Systema Naturae*, published in 1758, included eighty-five new insect species. Linnaeus gave credit to Rolander for their discovery but renamed each and every one.

Despite the rift, Abraham Bäck, Linnaeus's best friend and the king's physician, hired Rolander to direct Stockholm hospital's new botanical garden. But after a number of jobs and help from another of Linnaeus's former students, Rolander still couldn't make a go of his career. He floundered for the rest of his life and never published the seven-hundred-page manuscript he had prepared about his research in Suriname.

Linnaeus named a small beetle *Aphanus rolandri*. The genus name *Aphanus* came from the Greek meaning "invisible." Unfortunately, Rolander's good work went unnoticed for years and was finally published in 2008.

◇◇◇

Pehr Forsskål had already made a serious study of coral reefs near his home in Finland when as a ten-year-old he enrolled himself at Uppsala University. Seventeen years later, while studying with Linnaeus, he wrote a controversial pamphlet about civil liberty and freedom of expression and of the press, which was censured by the political party in power. Linnaeus helped him land a professorship in Denmark. Forsskål sailed on a Danish ship with a scientific expedition to the Sinai Peninsula. He explored Egypt, the Arabian coast of the Red Sea, and Yemen, where he found ninety new species of fish and thirty new genera of plants, and sent many plants home to his professor. Sadly, one after the other, the crew and expedition members died. Forsskål died of malaria in Yemen. Only one expedition member survived.

Linnaeus named a tough plant after this tenacious and persistent young man, *Forsskaolea tenacissima*.

◇◇◇

Anders Sparrman first traveled as a ship's surgeon on a two-year journey to China. He was only seventeen. At twenty-three, after studying medicine with Linnaeus at Uppsala, he followed in Daniel Solander's footsteps, joining Captain James Cook on the English explorer's second circumnavigation of the globe in 1772.

During the *Resolution*'s four-year voyage, Sparrman explored South Africa, the Cape of Good Hope, New Zealand, Tahiti, and many other Pacific islands, as well as the icy southernmost continent, Antarctica. He was a skilled naturalist, friendly and genuinely interested in people, their languages, and their cultures, and devoted to Linnaeus. He wrote to Linnaeus from the Cape in 1775 that his botanical work was often interrupted by spears, clubs, and poisoned arrows. Sometimes he wrote plant descriptions with a pencil in his right hand, a pistol in his left.

The sloop HMS *Resolution* anchored near an iceberg while men in small boats collect ice blocks to provide a supply of fresh water on board.

In Antarctica, amid fog, howling wind, icebergs twice as tall as the ship, and beneath rigging trimmed with icicles, Sparrman and his fellow explorers drank to the health of his aging professor back in Uppsala. They ate salted meat and picked weevils out of their moldy biscuits. They shook snow out of the sails. When they had traveled as far as they could among the icebergs, they turned back. As the ship came about, Sparrman, showing his playful sense of humor, ran to the stern of the ship so that he could claim that he'd been farther south than anyone in the world.

Twelve years later, Sparrman embarked on another expedition. His teenage adventure to China was in the distant past now, and Linnaeus had died. This time Sparrman went to Senegal in West Africa. While many of Linnaeus's traveling "apostles" set off as students and returned seasoned naturalists, Sparrman experienced a different transformation. He was already a seasoned naturalist. He returned an abolitionist, adding his voice to those who wanted the inhumane practice of slavery stopped.

During three months of exploring West Africa's coastal environment for native plants and animals, Sparrman and his colleague, a Swedish mining engineer, were eyewitnesses to the brutal horrors of the transatlantic slave trade. They talked with slave traders, enslaved people, and several African kings. On their return to Europe in 1788, they testified about what they had seen in Senegal at a government inquiry before the British Board of Trade in London.

Sparrman, a medical doctor, explained that the French Senegal Company's director had asked him to examine some prisoners in the company's dungeons. Dr. Sparrman found the captives desperate and their conditions miserable. His testimony was summarized in the hearing record:

> The slaves he [Sparrman] saw expressed the greatest Concern and Apprehension at the Loss of their Liberty. Many of those he witnessed in his physical Capacity, on his feeling their Pulse and examining them, trembled with Fear, thinking he was a Purchaser, and would send them to the Islands, which they dread.

Sparrman's fellow traveler had accompanied him into the dungeons. "Their situation was very pitiful," he told the British

House of Commons, ". . . particularly one, who was lying in his blood, which flowed from a wound from a ball [bullet] in his shoulder."

In addition to describing the atrocities by slave traders, the two Swedes praised the Africans' economic development and their skillful cultivation of maize, sugar, tobacco, cotton, rice, and indigo—exotic plant crops that Europeans clamored for. Sparrman's colleague raved about the beautiful gold craftsmanship in Senegal: "I never have seen better made articles of that kind in Europe."

As curator of the natural history collections of the Swedish Royal Academy of Sciences and a practicing physician, Dr. Sparrman was known in intellectual circles. With no financial stake in the slave trade, he was considered an impartial and rational scientific observer. After testifying, Sparrman returned home to his work. Even though he'd played only a small part in the overall abolitionist struggle, his testimony swayed the committee and impressed William Wilberforce, a member of Parliament. Wilberforce used Sparrman's account during his campaigning, which eventually led to the Slavery Abolition Act of 1833.

In 1782, Carl Linnaeus the Younger named a shrub or small tree that grows in the open woodlands of Africa, South Africa, and Madagascar *Sparrmannia africana*. Up close, its dramatic clusters of white flowers with red and yellow stamens look like miniature fireworks.

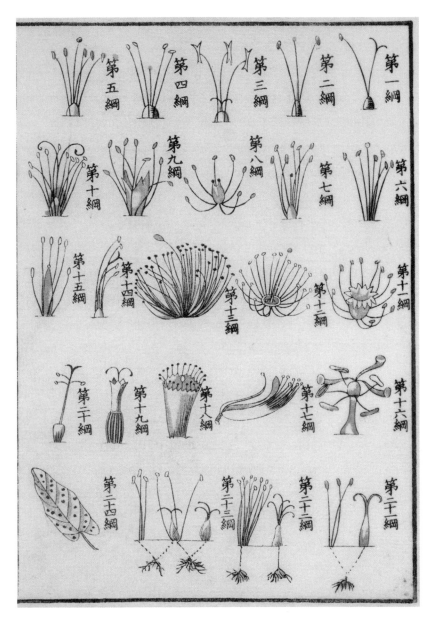

After Carl Peter Thunberg visited Japan, this adaptation of Georg Ehret's floral plate was published in *Shokugaku Keigen*, an influential 1837 book which introduced Linnaeus's plant classification system to Japan.

The last "apostle," Carl Peter Thunberg, explored South Africa, Sri Lanka, and Indonesia, and was the first Western naturalist to visit Japan in a hundred years. He learned about Japanese plants and medicine and taught Western medicine to Japanese practitioners in 1775 and 1776. He was so successful in spreading the Linnaean system there that his fame has endured. During the 2007 celebrations of Linnaeus's three-hundredth birthday, the Japanese emperor, himself a university-trained marine scientist, visited Sweden to pay his respects to Thunberg's teacher.

That generation of Linnaeans grew into independent, creative scientists. These "comets amongst the stars" opened doors for "comets" in the next generation.

11

◇◇

THE PROFESSOR

If a tree dies, plant another in its place.
—CARL LINNAEUS, LAST WILL AND TESTAMENT

An old man browsed in an Uppsala bookshop. According to a German botany student who was new in town that day, the man was shabby and unshaven, of average height. His shoes and stockings were dusty from the road. A medallion was pinned to his "ancient green jacket." The medal, the Knighthood of the Polar Star, had been awarded by King Adolf Fredrik to the world-famous Carl Linnaeus. He wore it every day.

That September day in 1765, Linnaeus had just returned to the university for the start of the fall semester. International students, like the one in the bookshop, often rented rooms in a house directly across from the Linnaeus family home. A couple of winters earlier, for instance, three of them—Johan Christian Fabricius and Johan Zoëga from Denmark, and Linnaeus's only American student, Adam Kuhn from Philadelphia—watched every morning as their professor, in his red coat and green, fur-trimmed cap, pipe in hand, hurried across the street for a short chat. These sessions rolled along for an hour or two, Linnaeus teaching, answering and posing questions, and laughing often.

These students fared well after their classes with him. Zoëga became a botanist, Fabricius a zoology professor and one of the century's most important entomologists, and Kuhn one of three physicians to teach at America's first medical college, now the University of Pennsylvania.

Outside of the school year, summer brought mosquitoes and stagnant, unhealthy air along the city's swampy river. Many residents suffered uncontrollable fevers and died from malaria. To protect his family, Linnaeus had bought a 200-acre farm estate called Hammarby in 1758, with a red-timbered farmhouse for his family and other houses for tenant farmers. From then on, they spent summers in the country, as well as Christmas and Easter vacations. (This would be the place where, after Linnaeus's death, Sara Lisa would live.) There, Linnaeus would rise around 4 a.m. and rush outside into the gardens in his nightshirt and stubbly beard. "Nature does not wait for powder and wigs!" he said.

With Hammarby a nine-mile walk from Uppsala along a dusty wagon path, Linnaeus's foreign students usually rented a farmhouse nearby for the summer. At 6 a.m., they would join him for breakfast, talking in Latin about natural science until mid-morning.

The whole family spent Sundays with the students at their lodgings. They hired a local farmer to play the nyckelharpa, a Swedish instrument played with a bow like a violin but fingered on a keyboard. In the barn, the students danced minuets and country tunes with Linnaeus's unmarried daughters. Every once in a while during an intricate Swedish dance called a polska, the energetic professor outdanced them all.

Also on Sundays, Linnaeus and his dog, Pompe, walked together from Hammarby to the church in nearby Danmark. Linnaeus often left in the middle of exceptionally long sermons, followed by Pompe. On occasions when Linnaeus could not attend, Pompe went to church alone, sat on the Hammarby pew, and left after an hour. The pastor complained, and Linnaeus teased that the sermons must be too long if even a dog would walk out.

In the yard at Hammarby, Linnaeus established a clump of *peloria*, the plant that had caused him so much trouble. He dug

Linnaeus's house and garden at Hammarby, in an engraving published in 1823.

unusual forms of other plants into the same garden, including a wild strawberry with strange leaves. Every summer he watched this garden flourish. Did he wonder when, or if, those odd plants would ever change into normal forms? Was he hoping to see bizarre curiosities arise from other species right there at his doorstep?

Gardens for teaching and research unfolded around the place. There were vegetables, apple trees, and fields of grain for making bread and brewing beer. On a hillside he called Siberia, he sowed seeds given to him by Catherine the Great, the empress of Russia. He planted a grove of trees which Lisa Stina's daughter, Sara Elisabeth, called "Grandpa's leafy bower" and where the family sometimes enjoyed dinner. He also grew a plum tree for each of his daughters, their family tradition. Cows grazed in the fields. He called them Summer-Rose, Fair-Cheek, Lily, and Blossom.

Inside the house, he pasted botanical prints like wallpaper. Hand-colored prints from Georg Ehret and others covered his bedroom walls. In his workroom, two hundred uncolored prints featured Caribbean plants drawn by a French monk, Charles Plumier. These had been sent to Linnaeus to verify the species' names before they were published.

When a fire destroyed a third of Uppsala in 1766 and threatened his home and collections in the city, Linnaeus began building a little stone museum at Hammarby. Unheated, with no fireplace or stove that could cause a fire, the building would house his priceless natural collections. At the top of a rocky rise away from the house, it became his "castle in the air." Its single room

Carl Linnaeus at age sixty-eight, wearing the medallion of the Knighthood of the Polar Star pinned to his jacket, in a portrait by Alexander Roslin.

contained his books and specimens. There were wooden benches for students and a "study-horse," a peculiar lectern-chair that Linnaeus designed. He straddled it when he taught. Overhead, the skin of a giant oarfish, the king of herring, stretched across the sixteen-foot room.

After he finished the last volume of his lengthy twelfth edition of *Systema Naturae* in 1768, life began to change for Linnaeus. Although his enthusiasm never dimmed, his memory was slipping. He was growing older, and his science was growing up. Most of his student-explorers had finished their travels around the planet; several had died during their expeditions. Trained by Linnaeus, they had discovered plants and animals and experienced continents that their professor had only read about. Already the world was moving on.

In the middle of a lecture in 1774, Linnaeus suffered the first of several strokes. He died four years later.

◇◇◇

Then began the transfer of power—Linnaeus's knowledge, his collections, his professorship. When Daniel Solander turned down Linnaeus's offer to be his academic successor, Linnaeus had arranged for his son, Carl, to step into the botany post at Uppsala. But Carl Linnaeus the Younger died of a stroke in 1783, and Linnaeus's last "apostle," Carl Peter Thunberg, was hired. During his explorations, Thunberg had become a well-respected botanist. Like others of the time, he sought to improve on Linnaeus's system of classifying plants by creating a truly natural one; his professor would have been pleased. However, Dr. Thunberg worked at a great disadvantage because most of Linnaeus's personal collections had been shipped off to England. Sara Lisa, needing money to support her daughters, had sold the collections to a wealthy young amateur botanist, James Edward Smith. The Englishman paid 1,000 British guineas for everything—a fraction of the value that Linnaeus had estimated in his will.

When the twenty-six crates arrived in London, Smith unpacked 19,000 dried plants, 50 stuffed birds in glass boxes, 150 dried fishes, 3,000 insects, 1,500 shells, 800 corals, 2,500 minerals, 2,500 books and manuscripts, and the three gray cupboards. (One of the cupboards was later returned to Linnaeus's house in Hammarby.) Smith discovered an unbelievable bonus tucked inside as stuffing. Linnaeus's frugal widow had padded the crates with a lot of old paper—thousands of letters from scientists all over the world!

Smith established the Linnean Society of London to house the specimens, letters, and manuscripts, making them available for scientists to study. The Society's meeting room quickly became an important center for scientific discussion. When a joint paper by Charles Darwin and Alfred Russel Wallace was read there introducing the theory of evolution in 1858, it received very little interest. However, a year later Darwin's book was published and sparked intense debates.

Today scientists from around the world continue to visit London to consult Linnaeus's own collections. They descend into the Linnean Society's climate-controlled underground vault to study the originals. They use his specimens as reference points in identifying species and as evidence of environmental change. In addition, high-quality scans of Linnaeus's handwritten manuscripts, letters, and herbarium pages are available online. These scans enable scientists to zoom in and examine minute details of the actual plants that Linnaeus himself described.

◇◇◇

During the 250 years since his death, Linnaeus has been hailed as a hero and scorned as a has-been. His systematic work resulted in a new field called taxonomy, in which organisms are grouped by their similarities, placed in a hierarchy, and given unique scientific names. Some biologists claim that Linnaeus, as the father of taxonomy, was merely a list-maker. They disregard the many ways in which Linnaeus contributed to science.

He brought order and clarity to the chaotic study of the natural sciences. He introduced standardized terms for talking about science, consistent rules for naming, and a basic structure to build on. Classification, or taxonomy, was never intended to replace botany, zoology, or geology. Just as a librarian helps writers and readers find what they need by organizing books, taxonomists help us see patterns in nature's bigger picture by organizing species. The librarian's work is necessary for literature. Taxonomy is necessary for natural science.

However, Linnaeus did more than organize. When he recorded the local names of plants and their uses by indigenous people during his travels in Sápmi, he pointed the way toward the twentieth-century discipline of ethnobotany, the study of people's traditional knowledge of plants.

During a 1745 trip to an island off the Swedish coast, he proved himself an early proponent of the science later known as dendrochronology. A recently felled oak tree prompted him to measure the widths of its annual growth rings. Later he consulted meteorological records and determined that the tree's growth had been greater during warmer summers and slowed dramatically during the summers that followed the severe winters of 1578, 1687, and 1709. Today's dendrochronologists use the growth of trees recorded in their annual rings to estimate environmental changes over time.

In addition, Linnaeus and his students, including Pehr Kalm who traveled in North America, advocated the wise use of resources and warned against excessive harvests of plant crops, animals, and timber. Another of Linnaeus's students composed a poem in 1762 asking a very modern question: "Why should we treat with contempt / and plunder forests and meadows / an inheritance given to us. . . . I deeply pity those who will be born a hundred years from now" in a world without forests.

Linnaeus saw evidence of the struggle for survival and the delicate balance of nature. He called the environment a "butcher's block" and wrote about competition as the "war of all against all." For example:

> There are some viviparous flies, which bring forth 2,000 young. These in a little time would fill the air, and like clouds intercept the rays of the sun, unless they were devoured by birds, spiders, and many other animals.

He also considered new ways to solve problems. For instance, he told students in a lecture that "until now no one has thought about exterminating insects with insects. Most every insect has its lion which persecutes and exterminates it; these predatory insects ought to be tamed and taken care of, so they can purge plants." He thought this would enable farmers to keep pests such as snails, caterpillars, and ants away from their crops. Today biological controls are sometimes used as alternatives to pesticides.

Throughout his travel journals and papers are astute observations that sound like twenty-first-century goals—conservation, biodiversity, and sustainable living. In many ways he was ahead of his time.

◇◇◇

Few people in the history of biology have looked so closely at so many kinds of organisms as that seemingly unimpressive man in the Uppsala bookshop. To organize all knowledge about the natural world, that man—one of the most influential botanists in history—broke the old rules of science and replaced them with new ones.

The rule-breaker became the rule-maker.

Carl Linnaeus was driven by curiosity and passion. He was a brilliant yet flawed man who helped to organize the way we think about the natural world.

Science is the pursuit of truth. Theories are the very nature of science, and they are provisional. They are always waiting for new data, for new tools, for new ways to be analyzed.

And, as Linnaeus understood, for new scientists.

Science remains a relay race.

TIMELINE

◇◇

1622—Johanne Pedersdatter (b. 1584), Carl Linnaeus's great-great-grandmother, is convicted of witchcraft and burned at the stake in Stavanger, Norway.

YOUTH AND EARLY SCHOOL YEARS, 1707-27

1707, May 23—Carl Linnaeus is born in Råshult, Sweden, to Pastor Nils Linnaeus and his wife, Christina Brodersonia.

1708, June—The family moves to the rectory in Stenbrohult, Sweden.

1711—Carl plants his first garden with weeds and wildflowers.

1714—Nils sends Carl to study with a tutor in Växjö, thirty miles from home.

1716—Carl enters the lower level of Växjö Cathedral School.

1717, June 10—In Paris, Sébastien Vaillant delivers his speech on plant sexuality.

1723—Nils tries to grow big pumpkins in his summer garden for his wife. In September, Carl enters the upper level of the Cathedral School.

1725—Carl receives a blank book in which he keeps his first notes about plants.

1726, September—Nils learns that Carl is failing his theological studies. Dr. Johan Rothman begins tutoring Carl in botany and medicine.

1727, May—Carl graduates from Växjö, eleventh out of sixteen students.

UNIVERSITY YEARS, 1727-35

1727, August—Enters Lund University.

1728, September—Transfers to Uppsala University.

1729, March—Meets Peter Artedi for the first time in Uppsala.
> **May**—Completes a handwritten work, "Spolia Botanica" (The spoils of botany), classifying plants from three regions of Sweden.

1730, May 4—Delivers his first public lecture as the botanical demonstrator. Prepares *Hortus Uplandicus* (The gardens of Uppland), a handwritten guide to the plants in the university garden and others around the province of Uppland.

1732, May 12–October 10—Explores Sápmi, crossing the Arctic Circle.

1733—Begins lecturing on mineralogy.

> **June 6**—Carl's mother dies.

1734, July 3–August 17—Explores the Swedish province of Dalarna, accompanied by students, to assess the natural resources for the governor.

> **Early September**—Peter Artedi leaves Uppsala for London.

> **December 24**—Arrives at Claes Sohlberg's family home for Christmas in Falun, Sweden.

> **Late December**—Meets Sara Elisabet (Sara Lisa) Moraea at a party.

1735, January 20—Proposes marriage to Sara Lisa in Falun. Visits his father in Stenbrohult.

> **April**—Departs Sweden.

YEARS ABROAD, 1735–38

1735, April 27—In Hamburg, Germany, examines seven-headed hydra.

> **May**—Leaves Hamburg.

> **June 13**—Arrives in Amsterdam.

> **June 18**—Registers at the University of Harderwijk, defends his dissertation on malaria.

> **June 24**—Receives medical degree.

> **July 8**—Meets Artedi unexpectedly in Leiden.

> **July 17**—Introduces Artedi to Seba in Amsterdam.

> **August 13**—Visits George Clifford's estate with Burman.

> **September 13**—Moves to George Clifford's estate, Hartekamp, as live-in physician and garden director.

> **September 28**—Peter Artedi's body is found in an Amsterdam canal.

> **December 13**—Publishes the first edition of *Systema Naturae* (The system of nature) in Leiden.

1736, January 24—Banana plant at Hartekamp blooms.

> **February 20**—Publishes *Musa Cliffortiana* (Clifford's banana).

> **August**—Publishes *Bibliotheca Botanica* (The botanical library).

July 21–late August—Visits England to find plants for Clifford's garden, tour museums, and meet naturalists.

September 3—Publishes *Fundamenta Botanica* (The foundations of botany).

1737—Publishes *Flora Lapponica* (Lapland flora), *Genera Plantarum* (Genera of plants), and *Critica Botanica* (The rules for botanical naming). Spends winter in Leiden classifying plants in the botanic garden.

1738, March—Publishes *Hortus Cliffortianus* (Clifford's garden), describing all 2,500 plants growing or preserved at Hartekamp.

April—Publishes Artedi's book, *Ichthyologia*.

May–June—Leaves Holland to return to Sweden, visiting Paris en route.

MEDICAL PRACTICE, 1738–41

1738, September—Begins treating patients in his new medical practice in Stockholm.

1739—Convinces Olof Rudbeck, director of the botanical garden in Uppsala, to hire Dietrich Nietzel, Clifford's gardener. Nietzel accepts the offer and moves to Uppsala, where he spends the rest of his life. Clifford never writes to Linnaeus again.

June 26—Marries Sara Lisa Moraea at her parents' home, called Sveden, in Falun.

1740—Publishes the second edition of *Systema Naturae*.

1741, January 20—Son Carl the Younger is born.

PROFESSORSHIP, 1741–72

1741, May 5—Appointed professor of medicine and botany at Uppsala University.

May–July—Leads a small group of students on a natural history expedition to the Baltic islands of Öland and Götland.

October 27—Gives his inaugural lecture, "An oration concerning the necessity of traveling in one's own country."

1742—Olof Celsius sends him a strange plant collected by a student. Later Linnaeus names it *peloria*, meaning "monster."

1743, June 14—Daughter Elizabeth Christina (Lisa Stina) is born.

1744, September 8—Daughter Sara Magdalena (Sara Lena) is born and dies two weeks later.

December 19—Linnaeus's thesis on the plant *peloria* is defended by student Daniel Rudberg.

1745, August—Publishes *Flora Suecica* (Swedish flora).

October—Publishes *Ölanska och Gothländska Resa* (Öland and Götland journey), account of his 1741 expedition to the Swedish islands in the Baltic.

1746—Crown Prince Adolf Fredrik gives Linnaeus a North American animal, later identified as a raccoon. Publishes *Fauna Suecica* (Swedish animals) and *Sponsalia Plantarum* (Betrothal of plants, in which he cites his 1723 pumpkin experience).

June–August—Conducts a natural resources survey of the Swedish province of West Götland with student Eric Lidbeck.

1747, April—Publishes *Wästgöta-Resa* (West Götland journey), an account of his 1746 expedition.

June—Publishes *Flora Zeylanica* (The flora of Ceylon; today called Sri Lanka).

1748, April—Publishes a revision to his early plant list, *Hortus Upsaliensis* (The Uppsala garden).

May 12—Father dies. Linnaeus suffers a deep depression as a result.

1749—Publishes *Materia Medica* (Medical material), vol. 1, and *Amoenitates Academicae* (Academic delights), the first collection of his student theses, 1747–69.

May 17–August 13—Leads students on expedition to study the natural resources of the province of Skåne.

December 24—Daughter Lovisa is born on Christmas Eve.

1750—Begins to call his students who travel the globe for natural science his "apostles."

1751, January 24—Daughter Sara Christina (Sara Stina) is born.

February–December—Publishes *Skanska Resa* (Skåne journey) and *Philosophia Botanica* (The science of botany). Describes and catalogs King Adolf Fredrik's collection of animals preserved in alcohol, stuffed birds, pinned insects, and shells in little boxes at the royal palace at Ulriksdal (publishes in 1754). Catalogs Queen Lovisa Ulrika's collection of shells and insects at Drottningholm Palace (publishes in 1764).

Linnaeus in 1747, smoking a tobacco pipe to dull the pain of toothache.

1753—Named by King Adolf Fredrik a Knight of the Polar Star, an honor awarded for contributions in science, literature, or other important civic work.

> **May 1**—Publishes *Species Plantarum* (The species of plants), the first known work using Linnaeus's binomial nomenclature system, which later is accepted as the starting point of modern botanical naming.

1754, April 7—Son Johannes is born.

1757, March 7—Son Johannes dies of fever one month before his third birthday.

> **April 7**—King Adolf Fredrik grants Linnaeus nobility (officially accepted in 1762).

> **November 8**—Daughter Sophia is born.

1758—Buys the country estate of Hammarby, about 9 miles (15 kilometers) outside Uppsala, adding two neighboring farms, Sävja and Edeby, the following year. Publishes the important tenth edition of *Systema Naturae* (animals, February; plants, June); the edition is later accepted as the starting point of modern zoological naming.

1759, January—Carl Linnaeus the Younger is appointed demonstrator of the Uppsala garden.

1762—Changes the family name to von Linné, after his ennoblement becomes official (Linné is the name by which he is still known in Sweden). Expands the house at Hammarby, which becomes the family's summer home. Nineteen-year-old daughter Lisa Stina publishes a paper based on her observations of nasturtiums.

1764—Suffers an attack of Uppsala fever, or malaria.

    July 12—Lisa Stina marries Carl Frederick Bergencrantz.

1766—Fire destroys a third of Uppsala, close to Linnaeus's house there. He designs a museum to house his natural history objects at Hammarby.

    May—Publishes twelfth edition (his final) of *Systema Naturae*, in which he deletes the phrase "no new species," acknowledging the possibility of the emergence of new plant species.

    July 28—Granddaughter Sara Elisabeth Bergencrantz is born at Hammarby. Later, to escape her abusive husband, Lisa Stina and her daughter move permanently to Hammarby.

1768—Queen Lovisa gives Linnaeus a pesky monkey named Grinn.

1769—Completes construction of the little museum at Hammarby.

1772—Retires from post of rector of Uppsala University.

1774—Suffers a stroke and is temporarily partly paralyzed. His health continues to decline.

1776, winter—Suffers another stroke.

1777, December 30—Has a severe seizure.

1778, January 10—Carl Linnaeus dies.

GLOSSARY OF BOTANICAL AND SCIENTIFIC TERMS

◇◇◇

Binomial—a two-word name

Botanist—a specialist who studies plants

Botany—the branch of science concerned with the study of plants

Bract—a small modified leaf growing directly below the calyx of a plant, or on the peduncle of a flower; sometimes larger and more colorful than the flower itself, as in the banana

Calyx—a whorl of leaves enclosing a flower still in the bud

Class—a group of animals or plants with shared characteristics, which comes between "division" and "order" in Linnaeus's five-tiered classification system

Classification—the arrangement of animals and plants into groups

Dioecious—having male and female flowers on separate plants

Embryo—in botany, a new plant developing within a seed; in zoology, an animal's unborn, unhatched, or incompletely developed offspring

Entomologist—a specialist who studies insects

Evolution—the transformation of animals, plants, and other organisms into different forms through changes over generations

Genus—a group of species having common structural characteristics different from those of any other group. Plural: genera

Geology—the branch of science concerned with the study of the earth

Habitat—the geographic area where a plant or animal naturally grows and lives

Herbarium—a collection of dried plants arranged systematically in a book, case, or room

Hybrid—the offspring of two plants of different species

Inflorescence—a group or cluster of flowers arranged on a stem

Mammal—an animal in the class Mammalia, characterized by mammary glands that secrete milk to feed the young

Metamorphosis—the natural process by which an animal or plant changes in form or shape

Monoecious—having male flowers that produce pollen and female flowers that bare fruit on the same plant, such as the pumpkin plant

Mutation—in Linnaeus's time, a change or transformation; today, a change in an organism's genetic material which may be passed on to future generations resulting in a new and different form

Nomenclature—a system of names

Order—a subdivision of a class which groups one or more genera sharing common features, ancestry or both

Peduncle—the stalk of a flower or fruit, or of a cluster of flowers or fruits

Pharmacology—the branch of medical science concerned with drugs and their uses

Pistil—the female reproductive organ of a flowering plant, usually comprised of three main parts: an ovary, a style, and a stigma

Pollen—originally, a fine powder; later, microscopic grains produced by a flowering plant

Quadruped—an animal with four feet

Rhizome—a horizontal underground stem which sends out roots and leafy shoots to produce new plants

Sexual reproduction—the creation of animals or plants which takes place by means of physical connection, and the fusion of two cells to produce a new cell

Species—a group of individuals sharing common features and/or ancestry, capable of interbreeding and producing fertile offspring

Stamen—the male, or fertilizing, organ of a flowering plant, comprised of two parts: an anther (a sac containing pollen) and a filament (a thin stalk which supports the anther)

Taxonomist—an expert who organizes living things following a particular order or arrangement

Taxonomy—the branch of science concerned with the systematic classification of living organisms

Umbellate—a mass of florets supported on stems of nearly equal length (called umbels) which grow out from a center, as in the plant Queen Anne's lace

Zoology— the branch of science concerned with the study of animals

NOTES

Many quotations appearing in this book are translations of their original Swedish, Latin, German, or Dutch texts. Full publication details can be found in Sources.

References to Linnaeus's correspondence are identified according to the system used by Uppsala University Library. Letters are also sourced, where possible, to Smith, ed., *A Selection of the Correspondence of Linnaeus and Other Naturalists.*

EPIGRAPH

7 "what all children": Yoon, *Naming Nature,* 5.

INTRODUCTION: SJUPP'S STORY

11 "If you do not know the names": Linnaeus, *Philosophia Botanica,* 169.

15 "obstinate as a knife grinder": Blunt, *Linnaeus,* 153.

16 "like a spider's web": Linnaeus, "Beskrifning På et Americanskt diur" (Description of an American animal), translated by Janet Anderson, emails to author, October 21–23, 2012.

18 "the one who scratches": Translated by Joseph Bruchac, email to author, May 10, 2017.

18 "really fine eating": Linnaean Correspondence L0840. Also in Smith, ed., *A Selection of the Correspondence,* vol. 1, 21.

CHAPTER 1: NOT ONE PUMPKIN

22 "though we be confined": Linnaeus, *Miscellaneous Tracts Relating to Natural History, Husbandry, and Physick,* 9.

28 "Brutal teachers": Blunt, *Linnaeus,* 16.

29 "If there is a single way": Linnaeus, *Notebook, The Transcription,* 7.

29 "The best medicines": Linnaeus, *Notebook, The Transcription,* 7.

29 "Many have not recovered": Linnaeus, *Notebook, The Transcription,* 7.

30 "Anyone who smears himself"; "Do not take the risk": Linnaeus, *Notebook, The Transcription,* 40.

36 "Is poor Carl to become nothing": "Linnaeus at School," Linné Online, http://www2.linnaeus.uu.se/online/life/4_3.html. Accessed July 21, 2017.

36 "a man learned, honest, mild": Linnaeus, *Notebook, The Transcription,* 187.

37 "to be medicus and botanicus": "What you enjoy doing, you will do well," Linné Online, www2.linnaeus.uu.se/online/physician/2_3.html. Accessed July 21, 2017.

39 "volatile spirit . . . breath": Vaillant, "Lecture on the Structure and Function of Flowers," 103.

41 "embryos with powdery feet": Vaillant, "Lecture on the Structure and Function of Flowers," 115.

CHAPTER 2: EVERY GROWING THING

43 "Minerals grow": Linnaeus, *Systema Naturae 1735,* 19.

46 "We immediately started talking": Blunt, *Linnaeus,* 29.

48 "I am no poet": Blunt, *Linnaeus,* 32.

49 "Preliminaries on the marriage of plants": Fries, *Linnaeus,* 46.

55 "the great inconvenience of copying": Koerner, *Linnaeus,* 40.

56 "the other would regard it as sacred duty": Blunt, *Linnaeus,* 30.

CHAPTER 3: INTO THE ARCTIC!

My main source for this chapter was the translation of Linnaeus's journal, *Lachesis Lapponica; Or, A Tour In Lapland.* All citations refer to this journal unless otherwise noted.

57 "Mountains upon mountains": vol. 1, 269.

59 "mathematical webs": vol. 1, 23.

59 "spar full of talc": vol. 1, 47.

59 "malignant beings of gigantic": vol. 1, 46.

60 "dreadfully bad": vol. 1, 16.

61 "as thick as a goose quill": vol. 1, 98.

63 "scampered away over hills": vol. 1, 97.

65 "a range of white clouds": vol. 1, 269.

65 "When I reached": vol. 1, 283–84.

66 "The lofty mountains": vol. 1, 289–90.

67 "lofty icy mountain": vol. 1, 321–22.

68 "In spring they eat fish": vol. 1, 330.

68 "They always let their boiled meat": vol. 1, 334.

68 "cram themselves": vol. 1, 332.

71 "half dead with cold": vol. 1, 158.

73 "[I]n other regions": vol. 1, 152. Smith's footnote identifies the fungus as agaric of willow, *Boletus suaveolens.*

77 "lowly, insignificant": Schiebinger, *Plants and Empire,* 202.

79 "absentibus parentibus", "called on S. L. M.", "explicitly solicited": Linnaeus, "Almanac," 7.

79 "A Lover's Farewell": Linnaeus, "En Älskandes Vale," translated by Ingvar Svanberg, email to author, August 18, 2018.

CHAPTER 4: DRAGON WITH SEVEN HEADS

80 "Many people said it was the only one": Fries, *Linnaeus*, 138.

82 "All this skilful man thinks": Linnaeus, *Musa Cliffortiana,* 16.

84 "watery bubbles": Linnaeus, *Lachesis Lapponica*, 1:262.

85 "A painter's invention": Linnaeus, *Systema Naturae 1735*, 29.

86 "if ever one has been seen": Linnaeus, *Systema Naturae 1735*, 29.

86 "After having been burned": Linnaeus, *Systema Naturae 1735*, 30.

CHAPTER 5: CAN BANANAS GROW IN HOLLAND?

91 "Dawn was always a friend": Linnaean Correspondence, L0059, translated by the author.

92 "paradise": Linnaeus, *Musa Cliffortiana,* 22.

96 "passed a miserable life": Linnaeus, *Musa Cliffortiana*, 157.

98 "a Monsieur Boerhaave, Europa": Blunt, *Linnaeus*, 95.

98 "These flowers did not all grow": Linnaeus, *Musa Cliffortiana*, 159.

99 "What is the meaning of honeyed liquid": Linnaeus, *Musa Cliffortiana*, 171.

99 "What is analogous": Linnaeus, *Musa Cliffortiana*, 171.

99 "like spiders' webs, white, parallel and tenacious": Linnaeus, *Musa Cliffortiana*, 171.

101 "a goddess of the ancients": Linnaeus, *Musa Cliffortiana,* 26.

101 "The pulp was very sweet": Linnaeus, *Musa Cliffortiana*, 219.

CHAPTER 6: NATURE'S BLUEPRINT

The account of Peter Artedi's life is based primarily on the biography that Linnaeus added to Artedi's posthumously published book on fish.

103 "We count the number of species": Linnaeus, *Philosophia Botanica*, principle 157. [Author substituted "count" for "reckon."]

105 "a lonely life, went to the tavern": Blunt, *Linnaeus*, 102.

105 "1. All things that are found": Linnaeus, *Philosophia Botanica*, 9.

105 "He kept me long, too long": Blunt, *Linnaeus*, 102.

106 "Nulla dies sine linea": attributed to the Greek painter Apelles of Kos (4th century BC) by Pliny the Elder. Pulteney, *A General View of the Writings of Linnaeus*, 17.

107 "If according to gross calculation": Linnaeus, *Miscellaneous Tracts*, 125.

114 "It is beyond controversy": Linnaeus, *Systema Naturae 1735*, 20.

115 "poisonous, stinging, sulphurous smoke": Fries, *Linnaeus*, 93.

115 "filled with steam": Fries, *Linnaeus*, 93.

116 "I feel dizzy": Frängsmyr, *Linnaeus*, 154.

116 "would gladly have believed": Frängsmyr, *Linnaeus*, 151.

119 "autopsy": Koerner, *Linnaeus*, 39.

120 "How Linnaeus Organized Plants into Classes": Adapted from the chart prepared by William T. Stearn in Blunt, *Linnaeus*, 248.

122 "lewd . . . such immorality": Blunt, *Linnaeus*, 121.

122 "ungrateful cuckoo": Linnaeus Correspondence, L0165, notation 4.

123 "every body ought to have them": Linnaeus Correspondence, L5624. Also in Smith, *A Selection of the Correspondence,* vol. 2, 174.

123 "When he was a beginner": Blunt, 105.

126 "He was generous with his praise": Blunt, *Linnaeus*, 172.

128 "perhaps the only lady that makes profession": Linnaeus Correspondence, L2194. Also in Smith, *A Selection of Correspondence*, vol. 1, 40.

128 "She deserves to be celebrated": Linnaeus Correspondence, L2051. Also in Smith, *A Selection of the Correspondence,* vol. 1, 39.

CHAPTER 7: LAST NAME, FIRST NAME

130 "The shorter the specific name": Linnaeus, *Philosophia Botanica*, 246.

131 "spineless stem": translated by the author with Carl George, email to author, September 7, 2016.

132 "an owl's nest": Blunt, *Linnaeus*, 148.

136 "An economist without knowledge of nature": Koerner, *Linnaeus*, 103.

142 "a clapper into a bell": Koerner, *Linnaeus*, 54.

143 "Names used by the ancients": Linnaeus, *Philosophia Botanica*, 246.

144 "are difficult to pronounce": Linnaeus, *Philosophia Botanica*, 214.

144 "liable to damage", "disgusting": Linnaeus, *Philosophia Botanica*, 214.

CHAPTER 8: MOST CONTROVERSIAL PLANT

151 "Fantastic . . . calf with a wolf's head": Gustafsson, "Linnaeus' Peloria," 242.

151 "Here is something remarkable . . . daffodils": Gustafsson, "Linnaeus' Peloria," 242.

157 "strange and unbelievable": Gustafsson, "Linnaeus' Peloria," 242.

158 "Nothing can": Gustafsson, "Linnaeus' Peloria," 242.

158 "[What causes] the transformation": Gustafsson, "Linnaeus' Peloria," 243.

158 "If with certainty": Gustafsson, "Linnaeus' Peloria," 244.

159 "Your Peloria has upset everyone": Gustafsson, "Linnaeus' Peloria," 243.

159 "[B]e wary of the dangerous sentence": Gustafsson, "Linnaeus' Peloria," 243.

160 "By careful examination": Gustafsson, "Linnaeus' Peloria," 244.

160 "Nullae species novae": Linnaeus, *Systema Naturae 1735*, 18.

161 "*monstre par excès*": Glass, "Eighteenth-Century Concepts," 231.

162 "the daughters of time": Fries, *Linnaeus*, 361.

CHAPTER 9: HUMAN VS. ANIMAL

163 "If I were to call man an ape": Broberg, "Homo sapiens," 172.

165 "There are none so delightful": VanHaelen, "Local Sites, Foreign Sights," 264.

165 "They are more amusing": Linnaeus Correspondence, L1613.

166 "If I knew how many teeth": Linnaeus, *Lachesis*, vol. 1, 191.

167 "No one is right to be angry with me": Broberg, "Homo sapiens," 170.

169 "Theology decrees": Broberg, "Homo sapiens," 166.

169 "I well know what a splendidly great difference": Broberg, "Homo sapiens," 167.

171 "grasp, sit, eat, threaten, [and] smile": Linnaeus, "Markattan Diana," trans. Ingvar Svanberg, email to author, October 17, 2016.

171 "mild eyes"; "Grech"; "Hoi!": Koerner, *Linnaeus*, 88.

176 "cousins of man": Nynäs, "Anthropomorpha," *A Linnaean Kaleidoscope,* 338.

176 "a second Adam": von Haller, journal editor, in an anonymous review of Linnaeus's *Fauna Suecica*, in 1748, quoted in Broberg, "Homo sapiens," 172.

176 "My vanity would not suffer me": Broberg, "Homo sapiens," 173.

176 "indecent": "Clement XIII, Pope," *New Catholic Encyclopedia*, Catholic University of America. New York: McGraw-Hill, 1967, 937–40.

177 "The absence of things": Linnaeus, *Philosophia Botanica*, 49.

178 "genealogical/geographical map": Linnaeus, *Musa Cliffortiana*, 58.

179 "there are somewhere apes": Schwartz, *Sudden Origins*, 59.

184 "Blow your nose!": Blunt, *Linnaeus*, 150.

184 "Step in!": Fries, *Linnaeus*, 258.

184 "Twelve o'clock, Mr. Carl!": Blunt, *Linnaeus*, 150.

186 "Linnaeus and Cuvier have been my two gods": Gotthelf, "Darwin on Aristotle," 4.

186 "I cannot at present give up my belief": Darwin, *The Correspondence,* 153.

187 "Expressions such as that famous one by Linnaeus": Gotthelf, "Darwin on Aristotle," 27.

187 "war of all against all": Koerner, *Linnaeus,* 83.

CHAPTER 10: STUDENT EXPLORERS

A thorough resource on all the apostles is Hansen and Hansen, *The Linnaeus Apostles.*

188 "A professor can never better distinguish himself": Fries, *Linnaeus,* 227. This letter praises young Rolander.

189 "army of botanists": Koerner, *Linnaeus,* 42.

189 "little birds that are shot": Koerner, *Linnaeus,* 42.

189 "Knäfvelen vet": Swedish Museum of Natural History website, http://www.nrm.se/en/forskningochsamlingar/botanik/botaniskhistoria/carlvonlinne.480.html.

190 "A table was spread for twenty": Blunt, *Linnaeus,* 169.

190 "house roofs in Uppsala": Koerner, *Linnaeus,* 42.

191 "hardly anyone loves him": Gribbin and Gribbin, *Flower Hunters,* 52.

192 "never failed to captivate": Blunt, *Linnaeus,* 154.

192 "he had the advantage": Blunt, *Linnaeus,* 154.

192 "If Linnaeus spoke": Blunt, *Linnaeus,* 154.

195 "on the hardest bench": Koerner, *Linnaeus,* 115.

196 "imitate nature in such a way": Hansen and Hansen, ed., *The Linnaeus Apostles,* vol. 1: "Instructions for Naturalists on Voyages of Exploration," 204.

198 "I often hear myself reproached": Robbins, *Travels,* 32.

199 "Hardly could we": "The development of protoecology in Sweden," Linné Online, http://www2.linnaeus.uu.se/online/eco/utveckling.html, accessed January 29, 2019.

200 "On both sides of this island": Kalm, "A Letter," 1750.

200 "Take fire-brands": Robbins, *Travels,* 153.

200 "almost melt in the mouth": Robbins, *Travels,* 168.

202 "Our Friend Mr. Kalm": Robbins, *Travels,* 152.

202 "Kalm's Account": Robbins, *Travels,* 170.

204 "sweetest mademoiselle": Blunt, *Linnaeus,* 193.

206 "your eldest daughter": Blunt, *Linnaeus,* 193.

208 "Economy is more of an obligation": Nyberg, "Linnaeus' apostles," 20.

208 "Fish breathe through lungs": Romero, "When Whales Became Mammals," 25.

208 "the brightest, strongest red": Greenfield, *A Perfect Red*, 3.

210 "greatly impressed": Dobreff, "Daniel Rolander," 12.

210 "As you know, for every creative spirit": Dobreff, "Daniel Rolander," 12.

212 "made me a present": Pulteney, *A General View of the Writings of Linnaeus*, 576.

215 "The slaves he saw": Rönnbäck, "Enlightenment," 431.

216 "Their situation was very pitiful": Rönnbäck, "Enlightenment," 430.

216 "I never have seen better": Rönnbäck, "Enlightenment," 431.

218 "comets amongst the stars": Fries, *Linnaeus,* 227.

CHAPTER 11: THE PROFESSOR

219 "If a tree dies": Blunt, *Linnaeus*, 221.

219 "ancient green jacket": Blunt, *Linnaeus*, 174.

220 "Nature does not wait": "Linnaeus the teacher," Linné Online. http://www2.linnaeus.uu.se/online/life/7_3.html.

222 "Grandpa's leafy bower": "Linnaeus's Grove," Uppsala University Botany website, http://www.botan.uu.se/our-gardens/linnaeus-hammarby/explore/garden-tour/linnaeus--grove/, accessed January 28, 2019.

222 "castle in the air": Blunt, *Linnaeus*, 241.

227 "Why should we treat": Koerner, *Linnaeus*, 83.

227 "butcher's block": Linnaeus, quoted at "Carl Linnaeus (1707–1778)," University of California Museum of Paleontology website, http://www.ucmp.berkeley.edu/history/linnaeus.html, accessed January 29, 2019.

227 "war of all against all": Koerner, *Linnaeus*, 83.

227 "There are some": Koerner, *Linnaeus*, 83.

227 "until now no one has thought": Koerner, *Linnaeus,* 83.

228 Science is a relay race: inspired by Mehmet Murat Ildan, *Galileo Galilei* [play] (Ankara: Republic of Turkey Ministry of Culture and Tourism, Art-Theatre No. 303–189), 2001. Email to author, January 14, 2019. The full quote runs: "History of science is a relay race, my painter friend. Copernicus took over his flag from Aristarchus, from Cicero, from Plutarch; and Galileo took that flag over from Copernicus" (trans. Mehmet Murat Ildan).

SOURCES

Many of the resources that I used, including some rare and historic books, are available online through Archive.org, Biodiversity Heritage Library, and various reliable websites including those of Uppsala University and its Linnaeus resource, Linné Online, http://www2.linnaeus.uu.se/online/index-en.html, and the Linnean Society of London.

Anyone wanting to read in detail about Linnaeus's traveling students should look to the excellent series from the IK Foundation, *The Linnaeus Apostles: Global Science and Adventure*, most of which are now available online at https://www.ikfoundation.org/ibooks/ibooks.php/. Another excellent and reliable site for specific information about species is the *Encyclopedia of Life*, hosted by the National Museum of Natural History/Smithsonian at https://eol.org/.

I have consulted many more books, letters, and scholars during my research than can be listed here.

LETTERS

The Linnaeus Correspondence can be viewed online at the digital platform run by Uppsala University Library in collaboration with other cultural heritage institutions, https://www.alvin-portal.org/alvin/ by searching for Linnaeus Correspondence, or by entering the specific letter number, for example L0165, in the search bar. These webpages link to summaries and to some English translations, which can also be found in Smith, ed., *A Selection of the Correspondence of Linnaeus and Other Naturalists*.

BOOKS AND ARTICLES FROM JOURNALS, SCIENTIFIC PROCEEDINGS, AND ONLINE SOURCES

Barthelmess, Klaus, and Ingvar Svanberg. "Linnaeus' Whale: a wash drawing of bottlenose whales (Hyperoodon ampullatus) at Hammarby." *Lychnos: Annual of the Swedish History of Science Society,* 2006, 303–17.

Blunt, Wilfrid. *Linnaeus: The Compleat Naturalist.* Princeton: Princeton University Press, 2001.

Broberg, Gunnar. "The Broken Circle." In *The Quantifying Spirit in the Eighteenth Century*, edited by Tore Frängsmyr, J. L. Heilbron, and Robin E. Rider, 45–73. Berkeley: University of California Press, 1990.

———. "The Dragonslayer." *TijdSchrift voor Skandinavistiek* 29, no. 1, 29–43 (2008). Available at http://rjh.ub.rug.nl/tvs/article/viewFile/10739/8310.

———. "Homo sapiens: Linnaeus's Classification of Man." In *Linnaeus: The Man and His Work*, edited by Tore Frängsmyr, 156–94. Canton, MA: Watson, 1994.

———. "Petrus Artedi in His Swedish Context." In *Proceedings of the Fifth Congress of European Ichthyologists, 1985,* 11–15. Stockholm: Swedish Museum of Natural History, 1987.

Charmantier, Isabelle. "Carl Linnaeus and the Visual Representation of Nature." *Historical Studies in the Natural Sciences* 41, no. 4, 365–404 (2011).

———, and Staffan Müller-Wille. "Carl Linnaeus's Botanical Paper Slips (1767–1773)." *Intellectual History Review* 24, no. 2 (2014): 215–38.

Coen, Enrico. *The Art of Genes: How Organisms Makes Themselves.* New York: Oxford University Press, 2000.

Colden, Jane. *Botanic Manuscript of Jane Colden, 1724–1766: First Woman Botanist of Colonial America.* Edited by H. W. Rickett and Elizabeth C. Hall. New York: Chanticleer Press, 1963.

Dalman, Margareta Nisser. "What's More Important, a Good Story or a True Story?: The merging of facts and fiction at Linnaeus' houses in Uppsala." In Mary J. Morris and Leonie Berwick, eds., *The Linnaean Legacy: Three Centuries After His Birth.* Special Issue no. 8, 27–34. Oxford: Wiley–Blackwell, Linnean Society of London, 2008.

Darwin, Charles. *The Correspondence of Charles Darwin,* vol. 20 (1872). Edited by Frederick Burkhardt, James A. Secord, and Janet Browne. Cambridge and New York: Cambridge University Press, 2013.

Dobreff, James. "Daniel Rolander: The Invisible Naturalist." In *Systema Naturae 250: The Linnaean Ark*, edited by Andrew Polaszek, 11–28. Boca Raton, FL: CRC Press, 2010.

Forster, Johann R. *Kalm's Travels into North America*, vol. 2. London: Warrington, 1770.

Frängsmyr, Tore. *Linnaeus: The Man and His Work.* Canton, MA: Watson, 1994.

Fries, Theodor Magnus. *Linnaeus: The Story of His Life.* Adapted and edited by Benjamin Daydon Jackson. New York: Cambridge University Press, 2011.

Gibbons, Ann. "New Human Species Discovered." *Science,* September 10, 2015, http://www.sciencemag.org/news/2015/09/new-human-species-discovered. Accessed November 23, 2016.

Glass, Bentley. "Eighteenth-Century Concepts of the Origin of Species." *Proceedings of the American Philosophical Society* 104, no. 2 (April 19, 1960): 227–34.

Gotthelf, Allan. "Darwin on Aristotle." *Journal of the History of Biology* 32, no. 1 (Spring 1999): 3–30.

Greenfield, Amy Butler. *A Perfect Red: Empire, Espionage, and the Quest for the Color of Desire.* New York: HarperCollins, 2005.

Gribbin, Mary, and John Gribbin. *Flower Hunters.* New York: Oxford University Press, 2008.

Gustafsson, Åke. "Linnaeus' Peloria: The History of a Monster." *Theoretical and Applied Genetics* 54, no. 6 (1979): 241–48.

Hansen, Viveka, and Lars Hansen. *The Linnaeus Apostles: Global Science and Adventure.* London and Whitby: IK Foundation, 2010.

Harnesk, Helena. *Linnaeus, Genius of Uppsala.* Uppsala: Hallgren and Fallgren, 2007.

Heller, John L. "Linnaeus's Hortus Cliffortianus." *Taxon* 17, no. 6 (December 1968): 663–719.

Johannison, Karin. *A Life of Learning: Uppsala University during Five Centuries.* Uppsala: Uppsala University Press, 1989.

Jonsell, Bengt. "Linnaeus and his Two Circumnavigating Apostles." *Proceedings of the Linnean Society of New South Wales* 106 (1982): 1–19.

Kalm, Pehr. "A Letter from Mr. KALM." *The Gentleman's Magazine* 21 (February 1751): 16–18.

Koerner, Lisbet. "Carl Linnaeus in his Time and Place." In *Cultures of Natural History*, edited by Nicholas Jardine, 167. Cambridge, UK: Cambridge University Press, 2009.

———. *Linnaeus: Nature and Nation.* Cambridge, MA: Harvard University Press, 2001.

Lehtola, Veli-Pekka. *The Sami People: Traditions in Transition.* Translated by Linna Weber Müller-Wille. Fairbanks: University of Alaska Press, 2005.

Linnaeus, Carl. "Carl Linnaeus's Almanac 1735." Translated by Nathaniel Wallich. *Proceedings of the Linnean Society of London* 2 (November 1848–June 1855): 5–12.

———. *The Carl Linnaeus Notebook, 1725–1727.* 3 vols.: *The Transcription. The Facsimile. The Comments.* Transcribed and with commentary by Torbjörn Lindell. English language revision by Eivor Cormack. Edited by Lars Hansen. Whitby, UK: IK Foundation, 2009.

———. Beskrifning På et Americanskt diur" (Description of an American animal that His Royal Highness has given to the investigation). *Handl-*

ingar: Kungliga Svenska Vetenskaps Academien (Proceedings of the Royal Swedish Academy of Sciences) 8 (1747): 277–89.

———. "En Älskandes Vale" (A lover's farewell). In Theodor Magnus Fries, *Linne: Lefnadsteckning*. Stockholm: Fahlcrantz, 1903, 15–16.

———. *Lachesis Lapponica; Or, A Tour In Lapland, Now First Published From the Original Manuscript Journal of Linnaeus*. 2 vols. Edited by James Edward Smith. Translated by Charles Troilius. London: White and Cochrane, 1811.

———. *Linnaeus' Philosophia Botanica*. Translated by Stephen Freer. New York: Oxford University Press, 2003.

———. "Markattan Diana." *Handlingar: Kungliga Svenska Vetenskaps Academien* (Proceedings of the Royal Swedish Academy of Sciences), Stockholm: Lars Salvius, 1754, 210–17.

———. *Miscellaneous Tracts Relating to Natural History, Husbandry, and Physick: To Which Is Added the Calendar of Flora*. Edited by Benjamin Stillingfleet. Translated by F. J. Brand. New York: Arno Press, 1977.

———. *Musa Cliffortiana: Clifford's Banana Plant, 1736*. Translated by Stephen Freer, introduction by Staffan Müller-Wille (14-67). Ruggell, Liechtenstein: A. R. G. Ganter Verlag, 2007.

———. *Select Dissertations from the Amoenitates Academicae: A Supplement to Mr. Stillingfleet's Tracts Relating to Natural History*. Charleston, SC: Nabu Press, 2011.

———. *Systema Naturae, 1735*. Facsimile of Linnaeus's first edition. Edited and translated by M. S. J. Engel-Ledeboer and H. Engel. Nieuwkoop, Netherlands: B. de Graaf, 2004.

Mägdefrau, Karl. "Camerarius (Camerer), Rudolph Jakob." In *Complete Dictionary of Scientific Biography*. New York: Scribner, 2008. Available at Encyclopedia.com. Accessed February 18, 2016.

Manktelow, Mariette. "Teaching Botany Inspired by Linnaeus: Is it possible?" *TijdSchrift voor Skandinavistiek* 29, nos. 1 & 2 (2008): 154–80. Available at http://rjh.ub.rug.nl/tvs/article/download/10746/8317. Accessed January 28, 2019.

Müller-Wille, Staffan. "Collection and Collation: Theory and Practice of Linnaean Botany." *Studies in History and Philosophy of Biological and Biomedical Sciences* 38 (2007): 541–62.

———. "How the Great Chain of Being Fell Apart: Diversity in natural history 1758–1859." *Thema, La revue des musées de la civilisation* 2 (2015): 85–95.

———. "Linnaeus' Herbarium Cabinet: A Piece of Furniture and its Function." *Endeavour* 30, no. 2 (June 2006): 60–64.

————. "Systems and How Linnaeus Looked at Them in Retrospect." *Annals of Science* 70, no. 3 (2013): 305–17.

————, and Isabelle Charmantier. "Lists as Research Technologies." *Isis* 3, no. 4 (December 10, 2012): 743–52.

————, and Isabelle Charmantier. "Natural History and Information Overload: The case of Linnaeus." *Studies in History and Philosophy of Biological and Biomedical Sciences* 43, no. 1 (March 2012): 4-15.

————, and Karen Reeds. "A Translation of Carl Linnaeus's Introduction to General Plantarum (1737)." *Studies in History and Philosophy of Biological and Biomedical Sciences* 38 (2007): 563–72.

————, and Sara Scharf. "Indexing Nature: Carl Linnaeus (1707–1778) and His Fact-Gathering Strategies." London: London School of Economics, January 2009.

Nichols, Henry. "Linnaeus at 300: The royal raccoon from Swedesboro." *Nature* 446, no. 7133 (2007).

Nyberg, Kenneth. "Linnaeus' Apostles, Scientific Travel and the East India Trade." *Zoologica Scripta* 38, Suppl. 1 (2009): 7–16.

Nynäs, Carina, and Lars Bergquist. *A Linnaean Kaleidoscope: Linnaeus and His 186 Dissertations*. Uppsala: Hagstromer Medico-Historical Library, 2016.

Pieters, Florence F. J. M. *Wonderen der Natuur: in de Menagerie van Blauw Jan te Amsterdam, zoals gezien door Jan Velten rond 1700 / Wonders of Nature in the Menagerie of Blauw Jan in Amsterdam, as observed by Jan Velten around 1700*. Texts from the Velten album translated by Marianne Arentshorst. Amsterdam: ETI Digitized Rare and Historical Books, 1998, 31–53.

Pulteney, Richard. *A General View of the Writings of Linnaeus plus the Diary of Linnaeus (1762)*. 2nd ed. London: J. Mawman, 1805.

Ramsbottom, John. "Caroli Linnæi Pan Suecicus." *Transactions and Proceedings of the Botanical Society* 38. Edinburgh: Botanical Society of Scotland, 1959.

Robbins, Paula I. *Jane Colden: America's First Woman Botanist*. Fleischmanns, NY: Purple Mountain Press, 2009.

————. *The Travels of Peter Kalm: Finnish–Swedish Naturalist, through Colonial North America, 1748–1751*. Fleischmanns, NY: Purple Mountain Press, 2007.

Romero, Aldemaro. "When Whales Became Mammals: The scientific journey of cetaceans from fish to mammals in the history of science." In *New Approaches to the Study of Marine Mammals*. Rijeka, Croatia: InTech, 2012. Accessed at http://www.aromerojr.net/Publications/669B.Book.pdf on December 31, 2018.

Rönnbäck, Klas. "Enlightenment, Scientific Exploration and Abolitionism: Anders Sparrman's and Carl Bernhard Wadstrom's colonial encounters in Senegal, 1787–1788, and the British abolitionist movement." *Slavery and Abolition* 34, no. 3 (September 2013): 425–45.

Schiebinger, Londa. *Plants and Empire: Colonial Bioprospecting in the Atlantic World.* Cambridge, MA: Harvard University Press, 2007.

Schwartz, Jeffrey H. *Sudden Origins: Fossils, Genes, and the Emergence of Species.* New York: Wiley and Sons, 1999.

Shuker, Karl P. N. *The Hidden Powers of Animals: Uncovering the Secrets of Nature.* London: Marshall Editions, 2001.

Skott, Christina. "Linnaeus and the Troglodyte: Early European encounters with the Malay world and the natural history of man." *Indonesia and the Malay World* 42, no. 123 (2014): 141–69.

Slezak, Michael. "New Species of Human May Have Shared Our Caves." *New Scientist*, December 17, 2015, https://www.newscientist.com/article/dn28687-new-species-of-human-may-have-shared-our-caves-and-beds/ Accessed January 29, 2019.

Sloane, Sir Hans. *A Voyage to the Islands of Madera, Barbadoes, Nieves, St. Christopher's and Jamaica*, vol. 2. Illustrated by Michael van der Gucht. London, 1725.

Smith, James Edward, ed. *A Selection of the Correspondence of Linnaeus and Other Naturalists, from the original manuscripts.* Vols. 1 and 2. London: Longman, Hurst, Rees, Orme, and Brown, 1821.

Stearn, William T. "Carl Linnaeus and the Theory and Practice of Horticulture." *Taxon* 25, no. 1 (February 1976): 21–31.

———. "Linnaean Classification, Nomenclature, and Method." Appendix to Wilfrid Blunt, *Linnaeus: The Compleat Naturalist.* Princeton: Princeton University Press, 2001. Appendix I, 246–52.

———. "The Origin of the Male and Female Symbols of Biology." *Taxon* 11, no. 4 (May 1962): 109–13.

———, and Gavin Bridson. *Carl Linnaeus (1707–1778): A Bicentenary Guide to the Career and Achievements of Linnaeus and the Collections of the Linnean Society.* London: Linnean Society of London, 1978.

Stoever, D. H. *The Life of Sir Charles Linnaeus.* Translated by Joseph Trapp. Whitefish, MT: Kessinger, 2010.

Svanberg, Ingvar. "Carl Linnaeus as an Aviculturist." *Avicultural Magazine* 122 (2016): 55–58.

Svenska Linnésällskapets Årsskrift (journal of the Swedish Linnaeus Society), 1956–57, 106–18.

Vaillant, Sébastien. "Sebastian Vaillant's 1717 Lecture on the Structure and Function of Flowers." Translation and commentary by Paul Berna-sconi and Lincoln Taiz. *Huntia: A Journal of Botanical History* 11, no. 2 (2002): 97–128.

Van Andel, Tinde, Paul Maas, and James Dobreff. "Ethnobotanical Notes from Daniel Rolander's *Diarium Surinamicum* (1754–1756): Are these plants still used in Suriname today?" *Taxon* 61, no. 4 (August 2012): 853–63.

VanHaelen, Angela. "Local Sites, Foreign Sights: A sailor's sketchbook of human and animal curiosities in early modern Amsterdam." *RES: Journal of Anthropology and Aesthetics* 45 (Spring 2004): 256–72.

Wheeler, Alwyne. "Peter Artedi, founder of modern ichthyology." *Proceedings of the Fifth Congress of European Icthyologists*, 3–10. Stockholm, 1985.

Williams, R. L. *Botanophilia in Eighteenth-Century France: The Spirit of the Enlightenment*. Boston: Kluwer Academic, 2001.

Yoon, Carol Kaesuk. *Naming Nature: The Clash Between Instinct and Science*. New York: W. W. Norton, 2009.

Zeveloff, Samuel I. *Raccoons: A Natural History*. Washington DC: Smithsonian Institution Press, 2002.

Zorgdrager, Nellejet. "Linnaeus as Ethnographer of Sami Culture." *Tijd-Schrift voor Skandinavistiek* 29, nos. 1 and 2, (2008): 45–76.

ACKNOWLEDGMENTS

Linnaeus was a "natural philosopher" (the word "scientist" was not coined until the 1830s). Like other natural philosophers, he had broad interests, so to write this book, I turned to specialists in many fields—botany, science history, zoology, wildlife pathology, ethnology, geology, even glaciology. I am thrilled to thank them all for being part of my hunt for the real Carl Linnaeus, for generously sharing insights and answering questions, and to several for careful critical review of my manuscript. Any mistakes that remain are my own.

I am most especially grateful to Gunnar Broberg, Lund University, for his thoughtful observations and encouragement, and Ingvar Svanberg, Uppsala University, for emails packed with information, and even translated passages.

Jesper Kårehed, scientific curator of the Linnaean Gardens, helped me imagine Linnaeus in his gardens. Isabelle Charmantier, head of collections at the Linnean Society of London, showed me Linnaeus's marginalia and note cards. Staffan Müller-Wille, University of Exeter, shared his expertise, including perspectives on Linnaeus's paper technologies. Charlie Jarvis, Natural History Museum of London, helped parse botanical particulars. Bengt Jonsell, Uppsala University, fine-tuned the chart of plant classes.

Carl George, Union College, Schenectady, New York, and Christine Cameron inspire me with their contagious curiosity. Charlotte Tancin at the Hunt Institute for Botanical Documentation, Carnegie Mellon University, Pittsburgh, tracked down answers and experts, and allowed me to handle (while wearing protective cotton gloves) books that belonged to Linnaeus and letters he wrote and sealed with his red wax stamp. Doug Holland and staff gave me a tour of the Missouri Botanical Garden's fascinating rare books collection, a place to stay, and a link to the Biodiversity Heritage Library.

In Sami, it's *giitu*. Thank you to Marie Enoksson, communications officer for the Sami Parliament of Sweden, for her helpful review of the Sápmi chapter; Janet S. Anderson, who translated Linnaeus's dissection report; pathologists Kevin Hynes and Joe Okoniewski, who allowed me to observe their necropsy of a raccoon; Torbjörn Lindell, Växjö science teacher, who knows all about Linnaeus's student days; Rev. Dr. Trygve Skarsten, who explained Scandinavian church history; Inger Herland, Stavanger, Norway archive, who translated trial records; and a trio of wonderful women who helped hunt down one important image: Christine Constantine, Frederica Freer, and Gerda Rossel.

Thank you to Mikael Ahlund, Christina Backman (who convinced me there was a different side to Sara Lisa), Eva Björn, Lynda Brooks, Maria Buhl, Enrico Coen, Andrea Deneau, Gina Douglas, Daniel Douglass (for emailing me about glaciers while standing on one in Iceland), Rebecca Flodin, Anthea Gentry, Håkan Håkansson, Andrea Hart, Marika Hedin, Esther Jackson, Jeannette McDevitt, Steve McLoughlin, Emil V. Nilsson, Eva Nyström, Jeanne L. Osnas, Annika Windahl Pontén, Paula Ivaska Robbins, Mary Sears (for help from the Harvard Library, above and beyond), Jennie Erin Smith (for her generous long-term loan of IK Foundation books), Angela Todd (who kept things light with Linnaean limerick writing) and Vivi Vajda (for reviewing the geology section); as well as scholars from the international C18-L listserv on the Long Eighteenth Century and the Linnaean Correspondence Project.

The world is a better place thanks to teachers who introduce children to nature—including Theresa Akerley, Alan Fiero, Jean Quattrocchi, and Yusuf Abdul-Wasi Burgess—and librarians who eagerly share their love of nonfiction, as my mother did.

My writing group by the sea is a talented crew, encouraging but demanding, serious but often side-splittingly funny: Deirdre Callanan, Pauline Grocki, Penny Haughwort, Maureen Hourihan, Sara Pennypacker, Ginny Reiser, and Jack Harrison. I am happy that my world includes terrific friends who give brilliant advice: Ann Foley, Connie Kintner, Steve Sheinkin, and Jennifer Armstrong.

Now to the publishing world. I am profoundly grateful to my extraordinary editor, Simon Boughton, who saw what this book could be before I did. He guided me in finding the right structure, then used his editorial superpowers on the result. Editorial assistant Kristin Allard (who is always sunshine), copyeditor Allegra Huston (who is always right), and the whole Norton team—William Willis, Rebecca Homiski, Tiani Kennedy, Jen Montgomery, Yang Kim—turned it into such a beautiful book. Heartfelt thanks to my agent, Susan Cohen, who believed in this project from the start and knew just how to shepherd it. Thank you all.

Special thanks go to my shared sister Patty, John and the ever-growing Figliozzi family for loving care and comedy.

And of course, my family, my favorite *Homo sapiens*. How lucky I am. My daughters and their husbands—Kim and Patrick, Kirsten and Dane—inspire and impress me every day. That they care deeply about the environment and the future of wild places keeps me filled with hope. The love in my parents' greenhouse and garden grows on in them. And Jim, by my side when I first set foot in Linnaeus's garden and ever since, you are my rock, my panini maker, my best friend, my favorite forester. You had me at *Acer saccharum*.

INDEX

ILLUSTRATION CREDITS